LEADERSHIP IS KING!

The one tool to help enhance your intelligence about leadership.

Sean F. Jones

ISBN: 979-8-9868538-0-2 (paperback)
ISBN: 979-8-9868538-2-6 (hardcover)
ISBN: 979-8-9868538-1-9 (ebook)

Library of Congress Control Number: 2022916372

Book Cover and Interior Design by TWA Solutions.com

Distribution by
Ingram Book Group
www.ingramcontent.com

Printed in the United States of America

Dedications

To my beautiful wife, Dana

Thank you for all the continual love and support you give our marriage, no matter the time of day or the mood of personality. No matter the struggle or the learning process, the fault or failure, with continued dedication you prove that we continue to move as a certified unstoppable force. There is no challenge too great. Team Jones!

To my mother, Ida Maria

First, I want to thank the seventeen-year-old you. It must have been scary, facing the challenges of being a teen mom, while in the process of learning about life, and while facing the tests of motherhood. Through your hard work and perseverance, you turned a GED into a college degree. You did a phenomenal job protecting and nurturing me. You provided me with the fundamental skills and morals to face and balance the depths of life. Thank you for helping me become a good man.

To my father, George

I am thankful for our relationship. Although we don't talk as much as we should, and we're sometimes in agreement and often in debate, I truly enjoy and cherish many of those conversations that last for hours. I'm always amazed at our similarities.

To my grandmothers, Ida and Ellanita

Thank you for loving me and truly making me feel that I could invincibly achieve anything. Most of all, for always teaching me to see the good in almost any circumstance.

To my siblings, Tiffany, Jamese, Mariyam, and Arielle

Although our different journeys in life has created distance, know that I walk with you all in my heart. There isn't a day that goes by where I don't evaluate my conduct and character against your thoughts of me as a big brother.

To my children, Jasmine, Ta-jai, Sameya, and Tori

Know that although our thoughts, paths, and ideas at times may differ, our energy is the same. You are special and filled with greatness. A seed produces after its kind.

Sending my sincerest love to you all!

Acknowledgments

Steven Anthony King*: Thank you for the talks and connections that continued to fuel this project. We don't talk often, but when we do, it's the talk of Kings!*

Victoria Christopher Murray: Thank you for all of your guidance and mentorship throughout this journey from the beginning. It was truly irreplaceable.

Jessica Tilles: Thank you for all your patience and for being such a consummate professional throughout the editing process. And thank you for bringing my book cover idea to life. *You have a great skill bestowed upon you!*

Thank you to all who have supported me in some way throughout my career and life.

None of us are greater than the sum of all parts!

Table of Contents

Introduction

*L*eadership is King, is a cumulative collection of thoughts, ideas, and interactions of my life experiences and relationships with leadership. It is inclusive of over twenty years of professional, systematic, and operational knowledge and experience in leadership—good, bad, and indifferent—in a world surrounded by politically and economically powerful people.

I spent twenty years in law enforcement in New York City, one of the most politically powerful and economically driven cities in the United States, if not the world. Within that time, I spent much of my career with the New York City Department of Correction, a place those unfamiliar with the agency's systematic makeup mislabel as Rikers Island. I spent a generation learning and understanding how to navigate within an organizational system that often existed with diminished and deprived resources. A deprivation that seemed to have created a phenomenal ability to persevere and remedy its own needs. However, like anything uniquely created and left without guidance and resources over time, can and will lose its way. There's a saying, "We the willing led by the unknowing are doing the impossible for the ungrateful. We have done so much with so little for so long that we are now capable of doing anything with nothing." There is also another saying, "Even the greatest love story will end unhappily if given enough time."

Within my career, I've had several executive positions, but one of the most important highlights of my career was the many years I spent with the Office of Public & Media Relations while working with the New York City Department of Correction. I had no idea how being assigned to that unit would change my life and all of those attached to it. I have had the opportunity to develop skills and resources that I've leveraged to help many of my peers—often unknowingly. Here, I learned that when you're in a position of power and influence, the people you help will most likely never be able to reciprocate, and you should not expect it. Not because they don't want to, but simply because of the roadblocks and lack of resources to do so. Here, I learned that leadership is a sacrifice.

One of the unique aspects of my years working in public and media relations was my professional interaction with countless celebrities and individuals considered prominent and influential in society which, to name a few, has stretched the spectrum from Billy Crystal, Robert De Niro, Eddie Murphy, and Denzel Washington to the Manhattan Madam Kristin Davis, Dominique Strauss-Kahn, Plaxico Burrus, and Lil Wayne. I've worked in tandem with some of the largest movie production studios on notable multimillion-dollar projects, such as *American Gangster*, and *Law & Order*, whose production crew I was once stuck in an elevator with at the jail in downtown Brooklyn, New York, for over an hour, only to be rescued through the roof hatch by the New York City Fire Department.

As a correction professional, who has risen through several ranks, I have had the privilege of being responsible for thousands of uniform and non-uniform staff, as well as those incarcerated. I have even had the favorable opportunity to be in the company of some of the greatest political and economic influencers of my time, such as David Rockefeller, former New York City Mayor and Presidential Candidate Michael R. Bloomberg, and many delegations and high-ranking dignitaries spanning the globe.

All the above-mentioned individuals share one thing: they have and, in some cases, are still leading masses of people either through their influence or decisions. Leadership exists in many forms and is evaluated in many ways. And to see it and its outcomes brought to fruition over the years lends to a remarkably invaluable perception of people and life.

Some live vicariously through people, while others can give life to the spirit of the masses through inspiration, motivation, and teachings. Although this can occur directly, often, it's with distance and in the grayest areas where you learn the most.

Being in the presence of so many influencers, whether through conversation or the observation of their energy, has heightened my consciousness and understanding as it relates to navigating within the plains of leadership. Many go through life believing you have to be like one of these people to be a leader. That there is something special that makes them who they are. Having been around many of these individuals, I can honestly tell you there's something special in all of us. The ability to be a leader is in all of us.

My focus and goal in writing *Leadership is King* was to ensure I gave back to the world positively by helping current and future generations understand much of what I have learned from experience by creating a literary blueprint that can help as an advanced guiding tool with the confusing plain of leadership. How to recognize what you see when facing leadership challenges and understand its outcomes.

What we must always understand is that although relative to one's perception, success in leadership will always require exposure and exploitation, as it is a greater place of sacrifice than reward.

No matter the circumstance, never allow your fear of failure to subdue your courage for leadership.

LEADERSHIP IS KING!

CHAPTER 1

Understanding Leadership

There are many interpretations of leadership. However, to be a leader, you must first be a follower. Before you can truly lead, you must learn to understand leadership. Growth requires awakening the leader within you.

This is a tenet of leadership and all great leaders of the world began this way. It is in the following where leaders are born and bred, and where leaders learn and grow.

Destiny is not by chance, but by choice. However, when you choose to follow, you must make that choice with purpose. Understanding your purpose as a follower makes you masterful when understanding your purpose as a leader. The process of leadership contours long before the leader becomes aware.

The military is a prime example of leaders beginning as followers. Every military leader begins as a soldier. Future generals learn to master the skills of high command and the responsibilities that come with it. The structure of the military incorporates the mass teachings of discipline. Equally important are the fundamentals learned long before the battlefield, such as understanding the importance of teamwork, time management, personal development, positivity, courage, and follow-through. These characteristics help to develop and promote a growth mindset and to make a great leader.

Studying great generals and their attributes reveals that courage is one of the first signs of leadership. The courage of leadership is an ever-sustaining variable in the unknown, and possessing it is primal in leading any group or organizational entity. Courage serves as the magnetic core for the complete development of success.

It takes courage to step into the role of leader. When you step into that role, you become like the character in a movie who says, "You guys go ahead, I'll stay behind." As is always the case in movies, that character is about to experience some traumatic event—possibly death. That is a courageous stance and what leadership is all about—Being willing to take the hits, making and understanding the value of the sacrifices, promoting the prosperity of the team, and creating and molding other leaders to carry on the mission.

Like generals, prominent leaders like Dr. Martin Luther King, Jr., and Malcolm X, displayed a substantial amount of courage. Neither of these men could walk down the street without a foul of animosity, a slur, an object, or excrement hurled their way. They were truly sufferers of heinous acts.

They traveled with bodyguards to protect them from harm. These men led change through courage and paid for change with their lives. It would have been so easy for them to have stepped down and out of the line of fire. However, that's not what leaders do. Leaders fall back on their courage.

Anyone exposed like they were on the battlefield of the streets, or even the corporate suites, is vulnerable. Being vulnerable and remaining in a position for the greater good is the courage of leadership.

Leaders, however, understand that courage is not the absence of fear. Courage is fear's combatant. Dr. King and Malcolm X feared for their lives, and at the end of their lives, their fear almost predicted their deaths. So, fear was there, just as it is there for the men and women in the military. By design, the rank structure of the military confirms this through implementing responsibility. As the rank and authority increase from officer to corporal to sergeant to lieutenant, and so forth, so do the vicarious responsibilities. Through the climb upward toward every level, there is a journey of courage you must take and conquer to rise to the next rank. As a leader, you must move past the darkness of existing fears to get to the next level.

A leader gains credibility by first being a follower. You can never forget where you came from. You can never forget what it was like to do the grunt work, to put in the time and effort, as well as make the commitment to move upward. It is in that process that you establish the marriage of credibility and integrity. Your history will show that you have been through the same things as the people who are following you now.

It is also in this process where you develop forward-thinking leadership, which is the understanding through practice that no matter the obstacle an organization or a person is facing, the directional agenda must continue to move in one direction—forward.

Now, one may presume they are moving forward, only to wake up and, after wasted efforts, realize they have been facing the wrong direction the entire time. Here lies the inherent significant value of the team. Forward-thinking is also about visionary planning, which allows you to anticipate the obstacles with enough strategic insight and mental momentum that not only will the hurdles be surmountable, but those who follow you will continue to do so and believe in you and the agenda.

The amazing leadership guru, John C. Maxwell, once said, "If you're a leader and no one is following you, you're just taking a walk." Many people want to brand themselves as leaders or in leadership roles, but these same people cannot cultivate or motivate people to rally behind them. Why is that? Why can some people step into a leadership role with willing followers while it is more difficult for others?

One reason may be that many see leadership as a thing, something that is static, when in actuality, leadership is an act of constant movement, constant change, and constantly moving people—it is a passion that one must believe in.

Leadership is less of management by the way of doing things the right way, and more of nobility by doing the right thing. It is the act of harnessing personal power and leading people in a certain direction, to do a certain thing, to attain a certain goal. It is a powerful thing when someone can influence and move people toward their vision. That is a leader. However, people in positions of influence, who are willing to trade their morals and conscience against a righteous cause to manipulate an outcome, are not leaders. They are being led.

Leaders...Born or Made

Are leaders born or made? Many scholars have debated that question for some time, and the debate will most likely continue into eternity. I am a staunch believer that everyone can lead and assume that position with the right background and the right lessons and have developed an understanding of their true purpose. It is important to understand that the greatest education, the greatest lessons a leader will receive, will never come from formalized education. Of course, some lessons will be learned in the classroom, but the greatest education will be life lessons that come through practical experiences. We have two eyes, two ears, and one mouth for a reason. The analysis of people, the development of social skills, the ability to see into the truth, and taking the time to listen are all phenomenal leadership characteristics of great leaders.

Ultimately, we learn leadership in its full dynamic through challenges. No one steps into leadership perfectly. You may have the ability, you may have the basic skills, and you may even have a natural talent. However, everyone needs refinement. A rare gem receives a lot of attention once people discover the reason for its existence, thus creating its value. There will be aspects of leadership that you may know and concepts that may be familiar to you, but no matter where you are in life, there are still lessons you must learn.

Everyone grew up or interacted with people who looked like they were born to lead. You know them—the phenomenal athlete, the girl who graduated with the best grades, the impeccably organized and well-put-together guy. They had all the talent and dynamics that made everyone say, "Wow, this person is going to go somewhere. They have the potential to be great."

However, if no one helped them to harness their gifts, if a parent, teacher, or another figure did not mentor them, if they did not have experiences where they could gain practical skills and knowledge, including learning through failure, then many of those thought to be elite will certainly fall shy of their presumed expectations. Without guidance and leadership, they will fall off, never to be heard from again because no one taught them, nurtured them, gave them structure, and inevitably never gave them the chance to learn the lessons of leadership that would have awakened the leader in them. One could say these leaders were born, but any spark that was inside of them was never ignited.

Then, there were those at the opposite end of the spectrum—docile as children, often dismissed to the idea of being great leaders, but through their journey and experience were later sparked into an outstanding leadership role. These people stepped up and into leadership after recognizing their passion and purpose because someone became their mentor, or maybe some experience set a fire in them and they learned the lessons, helping them to become extremely effective leaders. These leaders were made.

However, it is not just mentors who can teach lessons. One of the greatest "teachers" in life, especially to prepare you for leadership, is adversity. Having to go through situations and overcome trials can create powerful leaders, and these situations are the epitome of life's lessons. Adversity, which is any disadvantageous or unfortunate event or circumstance that happens, does not build a person's character. It **defines** it. When you find yourself in a negative situation and you must produce or perform under those conditions, that is when you find out who you truly are. You come to understand what you are made of and how you are built. When a challenge is in front of you, there are only two choices: you can fight, or you can take flight! It is obvious what a leader will do: step up, step forward, and do whatever has to be done to protect the missive.

Often, that is why people who come from the toughest of circumstances can become phenomenal leaders. Social standards may consider a man or woman to be rough around the edges, and not see them as possessing the social grooming to represent the stigmatized imagery and expectations of what a leader represents when, in actuality, it is because of his or her background. With the right mentorship and spark, a great and even phenomenal leader can be born. It all depends on that spark inside of us and what we do with it when it is lit!

Our lives are nothing more than the culmination of experiences, a multitude of paths that we must walk. Along the way, we choose how long to stay on a certain road, and what to do when we come to a fork in that road. It is inside these experiences and paths that we learn lessons and we discover ourselves.

For example, take someone who was born into a wealthy family. Both parents were doctors, went to the best schools, took part in the best social events growing up, and were exposed to the best of everything. Yet they became troubled, depressed, and even addicted to drugs and other social dependencies.

After hearing similar stories, we question, "How did this happen? How could you be born with all of that and throw it away?"

However, there are stories of the complete opposite. People whose parents were drug addicts, and because of the upheaval in their lives, lived all over the place—sometimes with their parents, sometimes with other relatives, or they didn't have any place to stay at all. Yet, under these adverse circumstances, they grew up to be highly respected individuals with professional careers—doctors, lawyers, dignitaries, etc.

After hearing this kind of story, we question, "How did that happen? How did someone overcome those circumstances and not only survive, but thrive?"

What is the difference between these two individuals? This is hypothetical, of course, but I would venture to say the person with wealthy parents had leadership skills within them, yet they never manifested because no one drew those skills out of them. They never had to face any challenges; never had to overcome much of anything. So how could the spark ignite? Where was their struggle? Where was their fork in the road? What decisions did they have to make? How could they ever discover their true character? If they never had to overcome challenges, how could their spark kick in? To sum it up, where were their lessons?

In theory, the person who grew up to be a doctor, to be a leader in their community, had to overcome all kinds of adversity, most likely daily. They probably had to make adult decisions as a child: where were they going to live? Would they stay with their parents? They faced forks in the road every day, having to decide whether to focus on their schoolwork or find a safe place to sleep. Their struggle was real. Their struggle was constant.

The path they were on could have led them to follow their parents. Instead, they envisioned a path that was so grotesque that it sparked them to do the complete opposite of what would have been expected. They used that negativity as their motivator.

It is difficult to become a true leader without adversity to teach the lessons and help develop who you should be. If you have never had any challenges to overcome, you will never know the fight or flight within you. Leaders find the spark within themselves. They use external experiences to ignite the spark that is already there.

The Strength of a Leader

Let us focus a little more on adversity. Phenomenal leaders result from the most difficult situations. Facing and having to deal with challenges is where a leader will rise. Adversity creates the best of who we are and who we are meant to be.

A question that at some point, each one of us will ask ourselves is "Who am I?" The way we handle adversity will answer this question.

Adversity reveals how we respond under pressure, and how we handle challenges by how we will react or perform. It is not something we always know ahead of time. We would like to believe that we know how we will respond to every situation, but the truth is we do not know. We will not know until we find ourselves in that position.

Imagine discovering a piece of coal has the potential to become a diamond. Who knew that pressure would turn something so ordinary into one of the most valued resources in the world?

Another example is a steam room. When the steam is turned on, engineers must stay on standby because the steam creates pressure that sustains inside the pipes. Once you turn off the steam, you ease that pressure, and once the pressure is gone, the pipe is no longer as strong as it had been. The pipe is not as structured anymore because nothing is flowing through it, and that could create many potentially unknown problems for the next time the pressure is reintroduced.

Using these pipes as an analogy, we see everyone does not have the same constitution. Everyone has different breaking points. Some break closer to the beginning of a situation, some in the middle, and others can handle the pressure to the end. Thus, everyone is not the same type of leader. Everyone does not have the same strength.

If you want to see the strength of a leader in everyday people, you do not have to look much beyond the ancestors of slavery. They survived the horrific and arduous three-month journey across the four-thousand miles that today we refer to as the Middle Passage. Then, once those who survived set foot on American land, they survived through centuries of oppressive hardship. Torture and torment were daily aspects of their lives. Even the end of slavery did not end the agony and anguish. They had to manage Jim Crow and segregation, lynchings, and all kinds of domestic terrorism. Once education was allowed, they had to navigate their way to school, walking tens of miles each way for an inadequate education because they were not allowed to attend white schools. They had to take ridiculous tests to vote and had to survive the humiliation of being denied jobs, housing, and other types of common opportunities just because of the color of their skin.

Under the white supremacy of America, the enslaved people were representatives of the strongest of pipes. With all that I just discussed, they stayed in the fight, and that is the lesson. If you stay, if you fight and do not give up, you will survive and overcome. There will be times when you stand and still lose. However, giving up makes losing a certainty, but getting up will turn that loss into a lesson. There is no winning in giving up, but if you stay, you will change the outcome and have a chance for a win. The person who wins is the one who starts by saying, "I'm not giving up." You must make that decision before any win.

This is the decision that a leader makes — either to be that pipe that bursts or to be the diamond that comes out of the pressure that has been placed on the coal. Truly, those are the only two options. If you learn to stand, you will grow. No matter the outcome, something will come out of it. Either you will get the results you wanted, or you will learn lessons that will help you face the next obstacle. Something good always comes out of standing for your convictions.

CHAPTER 2

The Characteristics of Leadership

Once the spark of leadership is ignited, there are so many aspects and characteristics that come along with that title. However, inevitably, leadership begins with your belief in yourself. That cliché, which is often stated, rings true: If you do not believe in yourself, no one else will.

There are leaders who come off as cocky for some people's tastes, but that is not always a bad thing. Leaders must not only be the first to see the potential in outcomes, but must also believe in themselves when others will not. They must believe in themselves when others may think they are a little off and a bit crazy.

Take Nikola Tesla. Many considered the Serbian-American inventor to be a genius, but there were others who wondered if Tesla's vision was really a delusion. In 1891, Tesla gave a speech where he said, "...our machinery will be driven by a power obtainable at any point in the universe." He was the first one to speak of this and even applied for a patent to have the world's first flying saucer because he believed he could harness kinetic energy. However, Tesla was neither respected nor valued for what he tried to do with energy. Very few had his foresight or insight. No one could see his vision, where he was looking at least one-hundred-plus years into the future.

The disbelief of others was of no matter or concern to Tesla. The leadership within him propelled him forward when no one else believed. Think about it—in the late 1800s, there was no value in terms of popularity or even much financial gain in what he did or in what he was talking about. He was way ahead of his time. However, what people said about him did not stop him. Still, he invented it. Still, he created it. He could not stop himself because it was innate. It was a drive inside of him; it was a spark that was ignited, and he had no desire to put it out. Having developed more than two hundred seventy-five patents in over twenty-five countries, he did it all not because he was a scientist, an inventor, an engineer. He did it because he was a visionary.

Being a Visionary

Leaders must be visionaries, looking toward a future dynamic that no one else can see. Visionaries have a looking glass into the future. It is important to note, however, that not everything a leader sees makes sense, especially when others are trying to see the vision with "today's eyes." Tesla wanted a patent for a flying saucer. The people at the patent office had to believe he was a little off. This was before December 17, 1903, when Wilbur and Orville Wright made history in their Kitty Hawk Flyer with the first powered flight.

Although people may laugh at an individual's vision, it does not matter to the leader. It did not matter to Tesla. The leader who has a vision has no concerns about what the vision looks like now. They will figure out how to get to the point where their vision makes sense. Not only will they figure out how to get there, but they will also convince other people to join in on their vision, even if no one else can truly see it. They will convince people to follow because people are always willing to follow a good leader, a person who can inspire them.

One of the most famous books in the world—the Bible— tells of another visionary, King Solomon, said to be the richest, mightiest, and wisest king who ever lived. Throughout, the Bible talks about his leadership skills, but the story that reveals his leadership the most is when he faced two women who both claimed to be the mothers of the same baby. When the two women were fighting over the baby, it was his leadership, his vision, and his knowing that the love of the actual mother would save the baby's life. Being both women claimed to be the mother of this child, and it could not be determined who was telling the truth, he declared that the baby be split in half. One woman immediately consented, while the other withdrew her claim to save the baby's life. He immediately knew who the true mother was when he foresaw the behavior of a mother who loved her child so much and who would never allow her baby to be cut in half that she was willing to give the baby away to save its life. His decision was bold, and his act was the sign of a phenomenal and intelligent leader.

A more contemporary visionary is Mark Zuckerberg, the technology entrepreneur best known for co-founding Facebook, who is in a constant state of being a visionary. When he was a teen, while kids his age were playing video games, he was creating games. Already considered a programming prodigy before he founded Facebook, he was developing and creating programs to help college students. He saw the future of computers when most of us were still trying to figure out the keyboards.

Leaders are visionaries who have eyes that can see things now so that others will see those same things in the future. They help shape the future with their forward thinking.

The Ability to Motivate

Motivation is the lace in the shoe of ambition, which is the energy that lights the path for others to follow. This may be one of the most difficult things for a leader to do, simply because it is difficult to get others to follow if they cannot see or understand your vision. However, as a leader, that is your goal: to get others to follow you! This is actually more important than the vision in the beginning—the prerequisite to establishing your vision.

A true leader knows that to move any agenda forward, the masses must understand the motivating factors. Leaders must always seek to understand the answers to these questions: Why should they believe you? Who does the vision benefit? What is the expected outcome? How does each person on the team fit in? If people do not feel or believe they bring value, or cannot see themselves under your leadership, they will not follow. Being clear about the who, what, when, where, why, and how influences followers' beliefs and makes the leader's vision more tangible. Having a better understanding of these questions helps to fertilize the seeds of motivation.

Understanding Opposition

Leaders cannot be winners if they do not understand when, where, and how they might lose. That is why a leader must know and understand their opposition. Take, for example, a boxer. There is not a boxer in the ring worth their boxing gloves who has not first studied their opponent. They have watched tapes and have learned their opponent's strengths and weaknesses because they would be a fool not to. It would be foolish to walk into the ring and not understand what they are about to face.

The same is true for any leader, regardless of the industry. You must know your opponent (or your competition) in order to win. You must analyze how this person moves and how they think. From the streets to the suites, whether you are in the bowels of urban society or a leader in the corporate world, the most successful people are those who analyze and strategize. Leaders do not make a move until they are knowledgeable about what their opponent will do. They do not take a position or any action without going through the process of strategic thinking and planning. However, the plans are not just yours. Leaders must always be conscious of the opposition at all times.

Filled with (Internal) Compassion

A leader must have compassion. They must have empathy and understand others in all kinds of circumstances. However, compassion from a leader must be more internal than external. The truth of the matter is the best leaders are not walking around, kissing and hugging everyone, nor do they need to receive that from others. A leader must be cautious and rare with the exhibition of compassion in showing paths of weakness, as compassion is sometimes mistaken for weakness; for it must be understood the weaker the shell, the easier it is to crack. The nicer you are, the more advantages people will try to take. That is just a human characteristic that a leader must understand; they must be fair, firm, and consistent. However, a leader must possess the ability to humanize all circumstances, especially those affected under their direction, and never place themselves above reproach.

If you are overly compassionate, you will not only hinder yourself, but you will handicap the people you lead. Everyone must have a standard of production, and sometimes compassion can impede that. No matter what your team member is going through, you must set a standard of expectation and excellence.

For example, if a teenager asks a parent if she can go out to the party of the year this upcoming weekend, the parent may say, "Sure, you can go, if, before the party, you've completed all the chores you were supposed to do."

Is that parent not being compassionate by not saying yes right away? Is that parent not compassionate because there were conditions and set standards? Of course, there is compassion there, but there are standards as well. Standards and expectations do not take away from compassion. Standards help people strive toward excellence, and that is what any good leader wants to do—help each person reach the pinnacle of their best ability.

Compassion is fine as long as the leader understands it must be worn inside a tough shell, and it comes with expectations.

Leaders Know the Art of Delegation, the Art of Praise, the Art of Fairness

In any organization, a chain of command is important to layout and delegate responsibilities. Delegation is the most intricate part of developing a system. For the system to be efficient and effective, a leader must not only delegate everyone a task, but they must understand their responsibilities, so they can perform the tasks with the most amount of accuracy and the least amount of controversy or failure.

For this to happen, everyone must clearly understand the system, its purpose, and the importance of their role within it. It is not enough for each team member to know their own function. For a system to operate dynamically and be productive, each team member must also know the functions of all who are on the team integrally. The team must know that no one part is greater than the sum of all parts, and, of course, this begins with the leader. The leader must be able to recognize the varying degrees of talents and abilities that exist within the team and delegate assignments accordingly. A true leader's ultimate goal is for the team to succeed, and delegation of responsibilities to the right people helps to maximize this goal.

Just as important as the art of delegation is the art of praise. Leaders understand the power and effects of praising and building team members up to recognize and encourage good performance. By the same token, however, leaders understand the equal importance of admonishing their team when necessary. With this understanding, leaders are always cautious with praising, admonishing, and knowing when to do each. Leaders understand the importance of praising in public and believe that admonishment should take place in private.

To add to that, I believe it is far more effective to praise and admonish the team as a team, rather than individually. By doing so, there is no direct assault toward one respective person, nor is one individual given all the credit. A leader can address the team because the team knows itself; all members know their strengths and weaknesses, and as a team, they will handle themselves accordingly. The team will work together to improve their weaknesses to do more than just survive. They will work together to strive. They will contour and govern themselves to achieve their goals.

The leader's responsibility is to organize teams that are cohesive and connected and to set the concrete standards for success. Once the leader does this and the team is clear on the goals, the leader has set the team up for success. Done properly, there will definitely be plenty of chances for praise.

Finally, the best leaders understand the art of being fair. Fairness is one of the most important attributes you can have as a leader because so many factors come into play if a leader is not fair. Without fairness in an organization, tumultuous and egotistical challenges will always arise. A leader must balance the tide.

Under no circumstances should a leader show favoritism. In most circumstances, favoritism will work against you. It may not be apparent at first, but leaders who show favoritism undermine themselves, and in the end, they are giving up their authority.

When people see favoritism, slowly, but surely, they will ignore the leader and funnel all of their energy toward the person the leader is favoring. Then, over time, that person can become the powerful one.

There is a great example of this in the book, *The 48 Laws of Power*, by Robert Greene. He uses the story of a king who did not want to do too much of anything beyond being a king. He thrived on just being on the throne. So, he made a man his assistant, called him the treasurer, and put him to work. The treasurer ran the kingdom, and the treasurer's responsibilities and power became very apparent at parties hosted by this treasurer in honor of the king.

These parties were lavish events, sparing no expense. Again, the king was much too busy to be bothered with the details of planning and putting these parties together. After all, he was the king. So, he beckoned the treasurer and gave him all the power and finances to organize these events. The king relegated his responsibilities to the treasurer.

For anyone to get into the party (as a supplier or a guest), they had to go through the treasurer, which meant that everyone knew the treasurer. Thus, it did not take long before the treasurer was the one yielding the greatest notoriety in the kingdom. No one mentioned the king. No one cared about the king. The king had unwittingly given away his power and notoriety.

What happened next? Jealousy set in. At the parties, the king noticed the treasurer's influence as everyone rallied around the treasurer. The guests would rave about how great the event was to the treasurer. Instead of attributing the shift in power to what he had done, the king blamed it on the treasurer. Jealousy is a powerful emotion that is as real as love, and, in this instance, it changed the course of the treasurer's life.

The king approached the treasurer with ire. Although instituted with the king's permission, the king still felt defied and betrayed. Without giving the treasurer a chance to respond, he locked the treasurer away to be imprisoned forever.

This situation came about fully because of the king. He was not a real leader. A leader does not defer responsibilities in that way. Leaders understand the responsibility stake being placed on their agenda, either directly or indirectly. For, by nature, the table of leadership is set with the duty of vicarious liability. A leader must know the difference between delegation and relegation.

With this explained, you must understand that fair expectations are equally important as fair consequences. There must be a balance between the two. People directly affected by the judgment, evaluation, and responsibility of the leader, who see that the expectations and standards are maintained, are more likely to be understanding and accepting of their accountability, and usually are more exemplary in their performance.

This will always serve the leader best by maintaining peace inside their organization. When there is an identified imbalance in the treatment of people within a team, either through privilege or accountability, that is when the leader's platform will crumble. Dissension and rivalry will set in and will become incendiary to the leader, which will be prevalent throughout the organization, from the workforce to supervisory positions, to management positions, to executives. Faith, followed by courage influences and supports the actions of the workforce, and that yields productivity and successful outcomes.

Leaders Leave a Legacy

Today, people drive vehicles manufactured by a company called Tesla, and many widely agree that King Solomon was a wise man. There are thousands of examples of this, where leaders have left a footprint on this planet, some decades, even centuries, after their passing. They have left a legacy.

The best visions outlive the visionaries because, as discussed earlier, most visionaries are so far ahead of their time. However, it may not only take time for people to understand the vision, but the understanding may also only come to others who are leaders.

One of the best things about visionaries is that they know who they are. Most realize they may not achieve their dreams during their lifetime. Instead, their only purpose may be in the sacrifice they make to just plant the seed. Leaders who leave a legacy do so without that being their intent. Their goal is to show others how to be their greatest. Legacy is understanding that the glory is not in the person, but in the actions taken and made toward the achievement of their intended goals. It is in these actions that we draw inspiration, even if the inspiration comes decades after the visionary has gone.

CHAPTER 3

The Look of Leadership

This may seem strange to say, but leaders have a certain look and I'm not talking about physically. It's a leadership aura. To best explain it, look at a leader and ask yourself: What is going on in their world? What is happening around that leader? What is that leader exhibiting? But most important of all: What do those under the leader's purview perceive that leader to be?

However, before I go more into that, I want to discuss image and the characteristics of a leader because those two aspects play an important part in what leadership is and is not.

First, let us discuss image. There are many who get caught up in their image. Appearance defines leadership, so many depend on the superficial: they dress to the nines and drive the most expensive cars. Some even determine their worth based on the square footage and the zip codes of their homes.

As you look closer at that person, you understand that maybe that is all they are: their clothes, their car, their home. In truth, you can see they are hollow beings because their shell is the only evidence of what they categorize as "leadership." There is no fruit in their lives. There is nothing growing around them. There is nothing inside of them. We all have tapped a hollow object and heard the echo—nothing of substance inside. This is the same for a person in a position of leadership, who is all image, and is challenged. That person, too, returns nothing of substance.

Then, there are those who go just beyond the superficial. These individuals have grandiose resumes, perform well in interviews, and make articulate presentations. However, those, too, can be nothing more than tools of distraction meant to hide what is not there. It is like spraying air freshener to mask a foul odor. Yes, for a time, the odor appears to be gone. However, once the air freshener dissipates (i.e., removal of the mask), the odor remains.

Human resources executives will tell you they have seen the shiny boxes, and then were disappointed with the gift inside. Yes, the box was beautiful, but it was empty.

Often, however, the expensive suit-wearing, grand-resume-carrying, articulate individuals remain in place in leadership roles because many of those who are in decision-making positions are similarly fooled by "shiny things." Big names and bright lights infatuate the masses, so it is easy to fool people with what's on the outside, even though productivity and results are what's most important.

The most important "attire" a leader can wear, the most important variable in leadership, is one's ability to perform—to get results and have a positive impact in the leadership capacity. The fact is, you cannot identify a leader by looks. A leader's best "evidence" is the fruit that is evident around them.

The fruit is always apparent in a leader's life. Their production is always obvious in the organization's health and the way the company and people are advancing. You must evaluate a leader by their body of work, their outcomes, and how many leaders they continue to produce.

Don't Miss Out on the Un-shiny Objects

Now, not that you should not be stylish, articulate, and present yourself well on paper. However, what the above shows is that none of that, alone, will ever create a qualified leader. An expensive suit will not produce results.

The bottom line is this: results are the only things that matter because results equal rewards. Let's take Albert Einstein, for instance. From pictures, the physicist, who was born in the late 1800s, didn't much care about his physical appearance. There wasn't much to look at on the outside because he wasn't a super fancy man. One may assume Mr. Einstein probably spent most of his adult life inside a laboratory, wearing some kind of lab coat. However, his physicality had nothing to do with the massive impact he had on the world of physics. What he looked like had nothing to do with his results. His body of work was phenomenal, and his impact continues today.

Leonardo Di Vinci is another person whose results had nothing to do with the physical package. He wasn't a shiny object. Although he appeared rather unruly, his body of work, from the "Mona Lisa" to the "Vitruvian Man," the first diagram of the human anatomy, are examples of Di Vinci's productivity that remains centuries after his death. His work exhibited all the substance of detail and culture that his physical attributes and aesthetics did not.

The same human resources executives I talked about above will tell you they've met individuals who didn't have much of a presentation, so their expectations were low. However, when given the chance, they were surprised at how well these men and women outperformed their peers.

It is important never to be fooled by the package. Do not be fooled by the one that glitters, and don't dismiss the one that does not.

CHAPTER 4

The Mind of a Leader

There is one thing about human nature: so much of what we do is the same, including the way we think. You don't have to look any further than the activities we experience every day. We incur a long line of some sort—at the grocery store or even a toll lane on an expressway. These places have one thing in common: there will be at least one long line and a short line alongside it. I always wonder why people are in the longest line, and why are they content to stay there?

The reason for this phenomenon is what I call *in-the-box thinking*, which is exactly what it says—we learned to think inside of a box.

Our institutional thinking began at very young ages. At the beginning of our schooling, one of the first activities we learn is getting in line. We stood one behind the other, not moving to the left, not moving to the right, because stepping out of line could have gotten us in trouble or danger, or so we were told. When we're young, we're taught to avoid danger at all costs. Then, as adults, we continue with what we've learned and always revert to the safest plan. That's why we stand in line, even when we don't have to, and many relegate to that comfort zone.

We learned it, we subscribed to it, and we accepted it. Everyone else is doing it, so we go along and assimilate within the herd. We're not encouraged to change our thinking. We're not encouraged to be individuals. We're not encouraged to be leaders, to be visionaries. If we're not taught to be leaders with a vision, that means we're followers without a purpose.

In Chapter One, I specified how leaders come from followers. So, going back to those lines in the grocery store, or at the toll booth, if everyone is on this line, this must be the safest place. This must be the way to go.

How do you combat this thinking? First, you must know you're thinking this way. Next, commit to thinking for yourself and stepping out of the box. Once you achieve out-of-the-box thinking, you will look at the long lines and say, "I don't want that. Why should I do that when there's a shorter line over there? Why should I expect to attempt to identify the intelligence of the person in the line before me? Why are they standing in that line?" Understanding and recognizing that you're thinking in the box is your first step toward getting out of it and becoming a strategic thinker.

It takes reprogramming your mind for this to happen, but the challenge is that this kind of reteaching will never happen in a standardized school system. Most standardized systems are too large to conform to an independent way of thinking. It is easier to teach the masses to behave the same way, to do the same things, and to think the same way. However, this relearning of how to think doesn't have to be left to our educational system. You can reteach yourself to become an out-of-the-box thinker.

It is important to note, however, that this is not a simple task. Stepping away from the herd mentality and thinking out of the box will always bring criticism from others. People will try to talk you out of "going over there," or make you feel inferior for seeking another way.

"It's too dangerous," they will say. "No one else is over there. There must be something wrong."

However, out-of-the-box thinkers know that "over there" is where they will find all the resources and opportunities. In the examples used above, the most valuable resource that is "over there" is time. Standing in the shorter lines will save time, which is one of your most precious commodities in the existence of mankind. Maximizing the use of ample, idle time allows for the further interaction and development of yet-to-be-discovered assets and resources.

The assets and resources may also be financial, experiences, or anything to help you grow. Going "over there" may provide opportunities for you to expand your business, learn something new, or meet someone who may provide you with a new endeavor. However, going "over there" can have risks, too. You may move to another line right as it closes. You may step out of the box and find that you took a chance that cost you both time and money.

Out-of-the-box thinkers know that wherever there are risks, there are rewards that are in direct proportion to how much you're willing to risk. Take a casino, for example. If you play the nickel slot machines, your reward will be a nickel's reward. Play a dollar slot and your risk-to-reward ratio will increase exponentially. The greater the risks, the greater the rewards.

That is how life works! There's an urban mantra used by many hustlers in the street: "Scared money don't make no money." There is also a commercial slogan for those who play the lottery that you must have "a dollar and a dream." No matter your walk of life, what is true is that you must be in it to win it. You must take the gamble. You must step out of the box! There is no return without investment.

What Box?

From what you have read, it may seem there are only two mindsets: to think inside the box or outside the box. However, there is a third mindset, one that can yield the greatest rewards for a leader. These are the individuals who do not believe that a box exists at all. These people will power toward success, mostly through their ignorance of not recognizing or understanding what most see as obstacles. Achieving success through ignorance is the best mistake you'll never make.

A great example of someone who never recognized the obstacles and did not subscribe to being placed in a box is Bryan Williams, also known as Birdman or Baby, the owner of Cash Money Records. Birdman grew up hard and rugged, coming into street hustling honestly. After a short stint in prison, he started a record label when the rap genre of music was expanding and becoming popular in New Orleans, Louisiana. Except for No Limit Records' owner, Percy Miller, also known as Master P, no one else had made a significant impact in that region of the country specifically centered on rap music; few had come out of New Orleans and made it to a national platform. Birdman set his sights on his home base and traveled to local clubs, recruiting artists. In just a few years, Cash Money Records had grown a contagious buzz, built a following, and his artists were selling significant units on the street. They were selling thousands upon thousands of units—a lot of movement out of the trunk of a car.

Cash Money Records caught the attention of several major record labels, and Birdman was interested in what they had to say. Even though he had been doing well on his own, he knew the whole idea in business was to use someone else's money, especially to expand. He understood the major labels had the marketing machine needed to take Cash Money Records from the trunk of a car and into the stores in the big cities. While he had made the original investment, he was ready to see his investment grow exponentially.

Birdman had several meetings with executives, and he walked into the door with his agenda. "Here is my product," he told them. "And here is the deal I want: 50/50 and I want to own all my masters."

While the 50/50 was tough enough, in this business, no one kept their masters. What he wanted was a deal that was unheard of. What both Birdman and the executives knew was that the money in this industry was in the ownership of the music.

Every executive looked at Birdman like he was a fool. They thought he was ignorant of how the corporate end of the music business really worked. He was told over and over, "We don't do that! No one in hip-hop gets their masters."

Whenever anyone told him that, he pushed back from the table and left. Every meeting ended the same way, with all the big names, all the big labels. No matter who he met with, he had the same demand: "I want my masters."

Their answers were always the same. "I'm sorry, but we can't do that."

Birdman stuck to his guns and went right back to work. He continued doing what made him successful: he recruited artists and kept selling and building that bigger and bigger independent buzz. Cash Money Records' fan base continued to grow, and music executives continued to watch. The executives knew he was doing something phenomenal because he was moving all these units by himself.

After a bit more time had passed, one publisher went to Birdman with a deal better than 50/50. "We'll give you a 70/30 deal," the executive told him. "But we cannot give you the masters."

Even those numbers were not good enough for Birdman. He still only had one thought: *I want my masters*. So once again, he told them no. He continued to say no until finally, out of the blue, one of the major labels called, and agreed to give him what he asked for. The Universal Music Group gave him a contract that allowed him to keep all of his masters, and a 90/10 split in his favor.

Later, Birdman would say in media interviews, "I did all of that out of ignorance. I didn't know that there were any rules. I just wanted to do what was best for me. I didn't know that I was going against the standard."

Birdman knew what he had, what he wanted, and he refused to budge from that position. He did not know a box existed, and most importantly, he didn't allow a box to be created for him.

This third way of thinking is the most important one for leaders—people who don't know that a box exists.

When I started in my industry, I would walk into a room, and, no matter where I was or with whom I was meeting, I saw myself as an equal. I never saw myself the way others saw me. Sometimes, they saw a newbie and sometimes they saw my physical attributes. All the time, they made assumptions and probably thought I should have been happy just being present. However, I always saw myself as someone who could not only walk into any room and be in step, but I knew I could change and increase the rhythm of the pace to my beat. I never cared who was in the room: money, status, fame. None of it mattered to me. I respected everyone, of course, but I demanded that same respect in return. I was their equal because of my level of thinking.

Although that may sound reasonable, that is not how the world works. Inside many conference rooms, the people in charge may not want you in the room. If you must be there, some may wish you to sit in the corner, remain silent, and never have a speaking part. When a newbie walks in and behaves as an equal, many will push back—hard! Some may even want to eradicate that new person because their thoughts are: Who are they? How dare they think they can come in here and walk equally in step with us? We've been here for years and we have earned this.

One thing is true: *you* will succeed at the level of *your* thinking.

Now, while there are times people will push back, there will be just as many times when people in the room will be intrigued when a new person walks in and does not subscribe to the rules. Leaders are impressed with those who are not afraid to step out of the box and even throw it away. Leaders recognize leaders.

That is how the world of leadership works. That is how power in business operates. When you walk into a room without even knowing or caring that a box exists and you function in a world of ignorance—in the most positive of ways—people will say one of two things: 1. This person is nuts, or 2. What this person has to offer must be the best thing smoking. I want that person to be a part of my team.

Again, you will succeed according to your level of thinking.

Success proceeds in that order: inside the box, outside the box, and those who operate as if there is no box at all. Leadership grows in those stages. In the beginning, you are in the box. Then, you step out of the box. Finally, you throw the box away. It is important for anyone who wants to be a leader to understand this process and evaluate its progress. If you want to be a true and effective leader, at some point, you must leave the box. Being outside and finally having no box and no boundaries allows you to grow uninhibitedly. The farther away you get from the box, the more you can venture into the world. The farther away you get, the more people you will meet, the more experiences you will have, the more connections you will make, the more failures you will overcome, and the greater you will succeed.

Ultimately, leaders understand that the farther you get away from the box, there are greater risks, but there are equal chances of greater rewards. In basketball, the star player gets the ball more than the others on the team. It makes sense. The team is trying to score to win. However, while putting the ball into the hands of the star gives a greater opportunity to score, it also gives a greater opportunity to miss. A star takes the risk because the focus is on the opportunity. Leaders, when given the opportunity, always shoot their shot!

Leaders Fly Like Hummingbirds

Birds are beautiful creatures that soar high above us. While they can fly high, they often fly together in groups patterned in a V-formation.

However, the hummingbird is unique because it defies the odds. The hummingbird does not fly in a standard formation. The hummingbird does not live, nor does it fly in a box. It does not understand that a box exists. It just flies. It can fly forward, backward, upside down, to the left or the right. The hummingbird defies all odds, and that is the way to soar as a leader—without inhibitions and limitations.

Forward Thinkers

Out-of-the-box thinkers do things in a forward motion. Those are important words for a leader. It does not matter what you do or what may get in your way. You must continue to move forward. Birdman had his plans. He had his meetings. When executives kept telling him no, he kept moving forward. Their decisions never stopped him. He kept signing artists and selling units.

People will look at Birdman today and say he is successful, focusing on his money, but money had nothing to do with it. He is a forward and futuristic thinker. He took a chance, understanding the rewards that came with the risks.

I am sure people wondered if Birdman was crazy, turning down all of those executives since so many artists wanted to be signed to the big major labels. There was a heavy risk with every decision he made. Every time he refused an offer, he risked no one ever being interested in him or his product again. However, he did what leaders do—stayed on his course to achieve his intended outcome. This type of thinking advances creativity, which is what forward-thinking is all about.

CHAPTER 5

The Strategic Thinking of a Leader

Leaders advance their steps constantly, always thinking about what comes next. This is an attribute I learned early on as a child from my mother. She taught me to think four and five steps ahead with anything I was doing. I was just a child, but she wanted me not only to think ahead but to think past any obstacles.

My mother and I would have conversations where she would evoke thoughts, so I did not stop thinking.

"Sean, what happens if the house ever catches on fire? What are you going to do?"

"I'm going to try to put the fire out."

That was a good answer, right? It was not enough for my mother.

"How are you going to do that?"

I told my mother about a fire extinguisher, and how I would do all the things she had taught me. Another good answer, right? Still, it was not enough for my mother.

"Well, suppose that doesn't work? What are you going to do after that?"

"I'm going to call the fire department."

She got me to think beyond the first obstacle, but that was not enough.

"Okay. That is good. Then, what will you do next since they won't be here immediately?"

"I'll get out of the house."

Once I was outside, you would think that was the end of it. Again, it was not enough for my mother. She wanted me to continue to plan. To think about how I would seek the help of neighbors once I was outside. She did not want me to stop thinking until there was no place else to go, there was nothing else to do.

This might be an extreme example for some, but in these lessons, I learned that most people only have one step, maybe two, in any plan. If those first two steps do not work, they either fall off the cliff or simply give up.

My mother taught me leadership and how leaders think ahead. How leaders are strategic thinkers, who constantly have plans in place. Every thought should start three layers deep. What if, what if, what if?

A strategy is an in-depth plan with not only all the steps outlined but also with built-in proactive failure response mechanisms that steer the plan continually forward to the intended outcome.

Successful strategies come in layers and must be planned. There are steps you must take to build out a strategy systematically and infinitely. You must chronologically lay out the blueprint in a step-by-step, phase-by-phase format.

The best leaders involve their teams in building those plans and the system. The team creates subsystems that build upon each other.

Typically, when people create their plans, they do not consider failure, only considering plans with A to B results. A strategic plan considers all outcomes and has a proactive response to consider intelligible obstructions or failures. The military and large corporations employ strategic planning officers. They deal with failure mechanisms, especially the major ones: what do we do if our original plan does not work? How do we move forward if something unexpected happens?

Like the military, we must have an alternative option—we must get to the intended outcome.

CHAPTER 6

Facing Failures

In Chapter 5, I talked about the best strategic plans having mechanisms built in for failure. A good leader will do that in anticipation because failure will happen. It is unavoidable. In many circles, people see the word failure as a bad thing. However, leaders understand that failure is part of the process. It is part of the leadership experience. Every good leader knows lessons come through failure. Leaders recognize the closer you are to failure, the closer you are to success.

Failure and success are often two sides of the same coin. It is like brilliance and insanity; any psychologist will tell you there is a thin line between those two. They are not opposites. They work in tandem. Therefore, many geniuses often become challenged socially and mentally.

However, it is often because of the fear of failure that people don't want to lead. They say they are leaders, but they want the title rather than the responsibility. You see this often with those hired to lead teams, and before anyone has blinked, the new leader has hired ten or twenty new people around them. Then, that new leader transfers much of their authority to the individuals they've hired.

A leader leads, no matter how many people they have in their organization. Leaders are hands-on, constantly getting involved with the team, understanding they alone are not the team but a strategic part of it, and that no one person is greater than the sum of all parts. Of course, the leader may not be a part of every minor detail. The leader is certainly not doing all the little things outlined in running an organization, but a leader has to be there with his or her hands on the pulse of the organization.

Can you imagine a police commissioner never walking the streets or interacting with the community? Not walking through the roughest and toughest neighborhoods? That commissioner does not have a real clue about what is going on. Without a clue, the commissioner will have no credibility, no connection with those they lead. And more so, no connection with the citizens they swore to protect. A true leader must understand the culture in which they are responsible to lead. Knowing the culture means having positive, open-ended, influential relationships with those surrounding them.

This is true of any business. The leader must stay relevant by being with the team, attending seminars, and networking with others in the industry. It may tempt you to relegate your authority and send assistants in your place, but that is the transferring of power. Just like in Robert Greene's *The 48 Laws of Power*, with the king and the treasurer; the leader will give the assistant the influence, the authority, and ultimately, the power. However, the vicarious liability of failure will always fall upon the leader.

Again, this happens when a leader is tentative and afraid of the failures that may come with the position. A leader is the beginning and the end—not God-like, of course. Those who look to their leadership will look for the leader to give ultimate direction and mature, calculated decisions. The person at the top cannot hide from issues or the responsibility of decision-making. The leader has a vicarious liability. Issues will locate those in charge like a heat-seeking missile. No one or nothing can shield the leader from the impact of whatever is to come. A leader must accept and take responsibility for every situation, every outcome. It is only with that acceptance and with the receivership of responsibility that anyone can be called a leader.

Here is the reality: as you rise in life, your ascension will come with greater chances for potential failures. The higher up you go, the thinner the air and the greater the potential for the fall. These things will happen to you and sometimes, the failures will be beyond your control. A leader steps up, makes the decisions, accepts the outcome, takes responsibility (with the team) for all the failures, and moves forward. That is the demanded expectation of performance. The flip side of that, though, is the leader, along with the team, will get the same level of credit for the many successes. Again, that is the demanded expectation of performance.

Fear of Failure Can Be a Saboteur

No one, in any industry, from politics to music, is at the top of their game, at the pinnacle of their success, and did not get there without experiencing tremendous failure. Failure is necessary because learning occurs with each failure. Success is often the end of the targeted motion and failure is often the continuance of it. Therefore, if you truly wish to succeed, you must face and overcome failure.

There is an old Southern saying: *Nothing beats a try but a failure.* Overcoming challenges with failure is easy: get up, dust yourself off, and try again. Learn the lessons and keep going! It is okay to look back from time to time, but only if looking back is part of your process and plan in evaluating your errors toward moving forward and being successful. The only thing that can hurt you is if you stop trying. Never, never, never give up! Never, never, never stop trying!

Sean John Combs, also affectionately known as Puffy, Puff Daddy, or P. Diddy, is a great example of this. He is a mogul in the music industry, but he didn't get there without his extensive share of challenges. Among them was an implication in an unfortunate stampede at a City College event where people were trampled and died and His friend and artist, The

Notorious B.I.G. was killed in Los Angeles. He was in the middle of that whole East Coast-West Coast controversy. Then there was the shooting in a club one night when he was with Jennifer Lopez. These are only the situations we know about.

Throughout it all, Puffy braced for impact and took it all head-on. He did not run from it. He faced forward and kept moving. It does not take much to understand that any of those situations that occurred could have placed him in a deep, dark place where no one wants to go, and when there, no one wants to sit with you. While Puffy was going through all of that, no one wanted to associate with him. No one wanted to be by his side. That is how it always is — the closest people to you will walk away from you. Some because they no longer see opportunity, and others because of self-preservation. As a leader, you may arrive in an uncomfortable place, facing your failure and wondering if you truly have the strength and leadership quality needed to make it through.

Even though there might have been times when he appeared down, Puffy was never out. He was a leader, and he knew one thing: if he stayed focused, on the other side of darkness was light. He knew if he could withstand those dark days, even more success would be waiting for him. Martin Luther King, Jr., once said, "Faith is taking the first step even when you don't see the rest of the staircase." Puffy took one step after the other without seeing the staircase.

If more people had P. Diddy's attitude, determination, and courage, more people would probably have his success.

The fear of failure is not a respecter of persons; everyone will face that fear at some point. I had to learn from my fear and failure. Admittedly, sometimes I allowed my fear of failure to stop me.

One day, while I was sitting in my office, I received a call from someone I didn't know. During that time, I worked in Public Relations for the New York City Department of Correction. In this capacity, I dealt with the media, dignitaries, and celebrities quite often, so that wasn't anything special on its own.

"Hey, my name is Bimmy, and I wanna talk about bringing LL Cool J to Riker's Island."

"Okay, you're talking to the right person."

LL wanted to talk to those incarcerated about picking themselves up from their mistakes and focusing on reforming their lives. After discussing with the higher-ups, and a few back-and-forth phone calls, Bimmy gave me some dates that fit LL's schedule. I got it all approved with the powers that be, and we brought LL to Riker's Island. He'd been there a few years before I had this position, and I was glad to have him back while I was there.

When LL arrived with Bimmy, I immediately felt LL's leadership. His energy was enormous. It was instantly clear why he was successful. When he arrived, he walked and talked with an abundance of confidence, yet he maintained such an astonishing level of humility. You knew he was supposed to be in the room. I've been around many celebrities and entertainers, but LL Cool J's energy is immediately felt.

I briefed LL and Bimmy, giving them an overview of the Discharge Planning programs we had on Riker's Island. Especially programs like the Fortune Society and Osbourne Association, where they provided services that would assist with reintroducing those released from custody back into the community before their discharge. These programs were important because they supported not only reentry into the community, but represented an opportunity to start a new direction, and an attempt to redeem themselves from past mistakes.

"All right," LL said after just fifteen minutes. "I got this. I can do it. Let's go!"

When he said that, I thought, *There's no way he is going to remember all of this.* After all, he had never heard of the information before. He had not had time to prepare, so how would he be able to repeat it, let alone promote it? We had given him a lot of information that was not familiar to him and had nothing to do with music.

But LL was a leader and, as he said, he had it. At that time, there were nine different active jails on Riker's Island, and LL did what I called the Riker's Tour. Over two days, he went to every jail and spoke to the population, using that fifteen minutes of information we'd briefly given to him. Every jail we went to, I gave him a little breakdown of the jail: high-level classification here, women here, etc.

After every bit of information, LL said the same thing: "All right, I got this. Let's go. Let's do this."

LL was right. He had this. He spoke at every jail like he had created the programs himself. Even though all of this was new to him, he embraced it. He did not know what he was going to see on the other side of the jail walls, but he embraced the challenge. He was forward-thinking and positive. He kept saying, "Let's go! I'm ready!" Never a shoulda, woulda, coulda, he just did it!

During the two days we did this, LL had a lot going on. He was producing a new album, filming a television show, had an extensive physical workout, and was on a no-carb diet. He would leave the studio after being there all night and meet me at Riker's at eight each morning. LL would spend the whole day speaking before he returned to the studio to start his schedule all over again.

It was unreal and unbelievable, but he made it happen. LL Cool J was an example of leadership. He understood his purpose, outlined and organized his plan, and met his commitments, all with the same level of energy and expectation.

I was extremely impressed at LL's relentless ability to tackle challenges in unfamiliar environments, and I enjoyed hanging out with Bimmy. In that short time, Bimmy and I developed a friendship. Now, I did not really know who Bimmy was, but even after LL's visits were over, we stayed in touch and even got together for dinner.

While checking in one day, I told him about an idea I had that came from one of my job responsibilities while I was working in the New York City Department of Correction press office. In that position, anything that was filmed in New York City that had to do with jail or prison scenes came through me. I worked on many projects, including television series like *Law & Order*, networks like HBO, and dozens of major films with directors and actors such as Martin Scorsese, Steven Soderbergh, Ridley Scott, George Clooney, Denzel Washington, and Leonardo DiCaprio, to name a few. While working in this arena, I knew there was a void. Independent filmmakers did not have the proper avenue to get the necessary exposure, and that's where my idea started.

"I've been thinking about this for a while. I want to create an Internet site for independent films."

"Oh, word? That sounds deep. Let me see the proposal."

"All right. The next time we get together, I'll bring it to you."

I kept my word and gave Bimmy the proposal. He seemed impressed with not only the idea but the way I'd put the concept together.

"Let me hold this. I'm going to take it with me."

"All right," I told him, thinking that he wanted to take the proposal and study it a bit more.

A few days later, he called me back. "Yo, I got somebody that's interested in this." He told me that the woman's name was Linda and she owned one of, if not the biggest, court reporting companies on the East Coast. "I talked to her. She loved this idea, and she wants to get together."

Now, this was when Netflix was just sending CDs in the mail. No one was really on the Internet, and streaming was something new. So, to have someone else able to see my vision, which I knew was forward-thinking, was exciting. So, Bimmy and I sat down with Linda and she loved the idea; especially since she frequented the Cannes Film Festival every year. She understood the concept.

"I want to do a deal with you," she told me. "I want to give you some money to fund the idea. I want you, Bimmy, and I to be partners."

"Wow!" I knew I had a good idea, but I was not ready for this. I wanted this. I believed in it, but I did not think anyone would have the same interest, and not so soon. At that moment, I learned something: we always want the opportunity, but subconsciously, often we do not expect it to come to fruition.

"Great," I told her. I was super excited!

Linda said she was working on some other things, but as soon as she wrapped them up, we would do the deal.

We continued to talk, and we had a few meetings, but as the weeks went by, the more tangible it became, the more we discussed the financial terms. She was going to invest a significant amount of money into developing this project, well into the six figures, which was a lot of money at the time for me to start an Internet business. I would be the one to manage the company. I would be responsible for all aspects of it. For the first time, I would be a business owner, in charge of my destiny, with no one else to blame.

However, I had not yet understood the power of fear. All that talk of money and responsibility made me out-think myself. All the self-doubt had set in. "No, I don't want to do it," I told myself.

The more I thought about it, the more I thought I could not do it. I was so nervous, and now I was too afraid to take the chance. I got in my own way with my fear of success.

I called Bimmy and told him, "I'm not ready to take that risk."

To this day, I will never forget what Bimmy said to me. He just kept repeating, "Don't be stupid." He kept reminding me that my idea was big.

Even though I heard him, and I knew he was right, I had done so much negative self-talk; I had talked myself out of it. I was too nervous to be successful. I was too worried about what I could lose rather than focusing on what I could gain. I suffered from the fear of failure, the uncomfortable place where success exists.

If I had faced my fears head-on, I could have been at the forefront of an exploding industry. I backed out of this deal because I was too afraid. I was in an uncomfortable place. I was at the door of success and was fearful of the unidentified thing on the other side: success! Leadership!

I was in a mental storm, someplace where I did not want to be, but I should have known what was on the other side of the storm. People always say, "The calm before the storm." Well, calm comes after the storm, too. The calm always comes again.

I allowed my fears to override everything. I lost out on a great opportunity, and now, I always use that experience as a lesson. This is one of my few regrets about letting my fear override my desire for success. Of course, there was the money, but there was so much more. I missed out on having a greater impact on the world. Yes, at times I still regret that decision, but I have carried the lesson forward.

CHAPTER 7

Public Opinion and Pop Culture in Leadership

As a leader, there is one thing to believe: public opinion is always an influential factor in how your organization operates. It does not matter if it is a private or public organization. You must be aware of the public and the opinions that come from the masses.

We have all seen it happen. Public opinion has taken down celebrities and politicians. Even companies have suffered under public scrutiny. People have lost contracts and endorsements. Public opinion can change not only a person's life but can challenge a company's bottom line.

Public opinion is so powerful because it partners with the media, whether traditional or in its rapidly growing current form—social media. With such a wide reach, social media can change public opinion in a matter of days, and sometimes hours. Sometimes, public opinion will come first and then the media catches up and catches on. Other times, the media will drive public opinion and influence the fall of a person or organization.

The public represents the politics of society; how the public sees you. The public's perception of you may not always be correct. However, perception is everything, and an incorrect perception could be detrimental.

The reverse is true as well. For example, a spokesperson for an organization gets embroiled in a scandal. The organization decides to sever ties, informing the spokesperson their services are no longer needed.

However, because of public opinion, it may not be that easy. If the spokesperson has a huge following, if they have support inside and outside of the organization, if they have what is called a power base, it will be more difficult for the powers that be to let them go. The organization may not want to face a public outcry, which could be worse than the original scandal. In that situation, public opinion may drive the organization to make a decision they would not have wanted to make, and maintain the relationship with the spokesperson. This is an example of when public opinion can work in an employee's favor.

It can go the opposite way as well. Public opinion can go against an individual. In the United States, freedom of speech is one of our rights. Our freedoms as Americans, and our First Amendment rights. However, understand this: not all speech is free because there can be personal consequences to what you say. Freedom of speech is not freedom of consequence. You are protected under your freedom of speech, but you have no freedom against the political or public opinion consequences and scrutiny that may come from that speech. You may say, "Well, that was just my opinion. I have a right to express my opinion." That is true. Everyone has that right, just like everyone has the right to disagree after hearing your opinion. The right works both ways.

The consequences that may follow a statement will not always be legal. However, the political consequences and public sentiment could be worse than facing an attorney. That is why leaders must take all of this into consideration. Leaders must think about someone speaking or writing and publishing content that could be offensive to a great number of people, of which the leader will have to decide if he or she will take that chance for the organization and risk destroying the results they wish to achieve.

This is an especially prevalent concern in the arts, with singers and writers, and even painters. Of course, you must allow for someone's creativity, because art is about being creative. However, the publishers of the art must be concerned about public perception, which will surely lead to public opinion.

Public opinion is so powerful. It can turn any and everything against you, so leaders must be extremely conscientious of what they verbally and physically represent. Shutting down everything because of public opinion is not the way to go either. Leaders must stand for something and must understand that someone is going to always take offense.

You never know who you will offend or what will offend them. So, a leader must be forward-thinking, anticipate issues, count the costs of how much moving forward will affect the organization, and decide whether to advance the agenda. Advancing the agenda for a cause is important, but timing is everything. That is politics, and will always come into play because it is the nature of an organization, a corporation, an agency—and people. There is always politics, both inside and outside the organization, and as a leader, not only do you have to be aware, but you must know how to move within the political structure. Politics and public opinion will affect your decisions, so in reality, you will never have a completely independent thought. You cannot. You must take into consideration who is who, what the powers that be think, what the implications down the line will be, and most importantly, how the bottom line will be affected because it always involves economics and achieving the intended outcomes. Leaders must move their agenda forward, but they must be strategic in doing so. And in doing this, the leader must make every effort not to allow themselves to be destroyed in the process.

Leaders Creating the Culture

While public opinion can shape people and an organization, the opposite is true as well. A person or an organization can influence the culture. What is popular predominantly influences all things in a culture. A phenomenal basketball player like Michael Jordan is popular, and then his brand, which includes athletic shoes and gear, becomes part of the culture. It is that way in sports, music, politics, and even in the corporate world.

The question is, however, who created the entire idea and concept of what would be popular? Who was the person who said, "These people are great, and we can do something amazing with them? We can create a brand!"

There are so many in our culture today: Kamala Harris, Jay-Z, Oprah Winfrey, LeBron James, Mark Zuckerberg, and even someone as young as Simone Biles—every one of these people has impacted our culture. Anyone with this kind of influence is most certainly in a leadership role.

Because of these people, created brands and products have changed, moved, and shaken world culture. Each of them has probably been told what they could not do. But as leaders, they were forward thinkers and risk takers and did not listen to outside noise.

These men and women dominate their fields because they are visionaries, even as children. In most of their situations, they did not move forward for money alone. Yes, I am sure they hoped there would be a financial gain, but that wasn't the motivating factor. What pushed them, what drove them, was their vision. Sometimes, the vision came from something that was about personal satisfaction, or they saw a void that needed to be filled, a problem that had to be solved. The money that followed was a benefit and a plus, a byproduct, but that was not the original driving force.

Take Warren Buffett, for example. Buffett, the American mogul, is one of the most successful investors in the world, and today he has an estimated net worth of more than $100 billion. This leader in the financial world did not start that way. He always had an interest in investing, but for his own personal goals. Even now, money is all relative to him; it is just a way to "keep score." For Buffett, money is a byproduct of his leadership.

It is not about the money for him. What is most important is about him being a leader in the financial world, helping people who are less fortunate, and trying to create a rising tide that will lift all boats.

CHAPTER 8

The Exit Strategy

A leader needs to know, even from their first day on the job, that an exit day will come and there will be an ending. In the law of success, any opportunity you have, any position you hold at a high enough level for a long enough time, will one day end. That is a fact of life! With that understanding, every smart and experienced leader eventually learns that having an exit strategy is extremely important.

This is an essential factor to understand because the higher a person rises in a company or organization, the greater, more strategic, and more consistent the attacks will become. The higher you go and the more successful you become, you will eventually find yourself in a battle with a formidable opponent for your integrity and credibility. No matter how much you have planned or how strategic you are, there will be a day when something you didn't, or couldn't have expected, will surface to explode faster than your ability to manage it. Your survival will depend on the body of work you have labored and developed and the people who believe in it, and who believe in you. Although this will come to make you stronger and more strategic, the wound from that battle will scar you, and you will always remember the fight.

This may be a little difficult to see when you first walk into a new organization as a leader. People who like you, people you have impressed, brought you in. You build a team, and all looks well. However, this is what you must know: as you are building, you do not just gather supporters, you also gather opposition. Leadership and success are magnets for all who come within their presence. When you hold the role of a leader, your opposition can become just as strong or stronger than your support. There will be a constant set of individuals who will lift you up, but there is always an equal and opposite reaction from the people who will want to bring you down. As a leader, you must be aware of and prepare for both. There is a saying, "Stay ready so you don't have to get ready," and this is true in leadership. You must learn to be prepared and brace for impact.

There are roles and opportunities that are not destined to continue forever. With this understanding, you can be extremely effective in steering and designing your exit.

Ask yourself the following questions: When Mad Day comes, when people you trusted the most turn on you, when the people you've allowed to access your inner circle decide to bail on you because they didn't agree with something you've done as a visionary, how are you going to handle that? How will you survive it, even if it means leaving? How are you getting out? What is your exit strategy?

I have had several experiences in my career at different levels. The further I went, the more I achieved, the more strategic I discovered the opposition, and the more I needed to be prepared to endure. This is serious business, as your career and livelihood are always subject to disruption. You cannot operate in leadership with blinders on. The higher you rise and the more you achieve, the more focused you must become to survive. The air gets thinner the higher you go and your pool of allies gets smaller. You must identify with your surroundings and develop an almost clairvoyant emotional intelligence that allows you to understand the movements of not only those in your environment, who you see as advocates, but also those who you identify as adverse and hostile. This is the only way to survive and see through the fog of contention. You must pay attention to energy, lengths of conversation, and, of course, those who hide thoughts of demise behind a firm handshake and a smile. There will always be signs, but they will not be visible unless you learn to understand them. This is an intricate part of being able to develop an exit strategy. You must be able to recognize formidable odds, and knowing that the facts of success will one day bring those challenges, you must allow yourself to see them as your motivator to stay ready for an exit.

As I made my plan, I kept something in my mind that my mother had told me. I was young when she said, "Challenges are going to come. And when they come, you must brace for impact." She also taught me to never run. "Running only gives the people coming after you time to think about how to deal with you. It is better to face it because the faster you cut off the attack, the better chance you have of surviving. But know that you are going to get hit, so brace for the impact."

One of the significantly formidable instances in my career was when I became the Deputy Chief of Staff for the Commissioner of the New York City Department of Correction. This is a very large law enforcement agency, which then had a massive $1.3 billion budget, within the confines of the largest city in the United States of America, with a population of over eight million citizens. The jurisdiction of the agency covered not only the infamous Rikers Island, but in addition, separate jail facilities in four of the five New York City boroughs, separate court holdings in each of the five boroughs, and once held an incarcerated population of close to twenty-two thousand. In my position, I had to deal with a phenomenal amount of politics that came with the job. I was the medium between the commissioner and the three main uniform unions. I helped facilitate the integration and development of policy, as well as assisted in developing plans to improve the existing jail's function and housing on many levels. I was required to analyze all jail data daily, update the commissioner in real-time on changes in the data trends, as well as respond to all types of incidents and events including deaths, suicides, homicides, escapes, drug overdoses, serious assaults on staff, stabbings, in addition to being the medium for all uniform union labor issues. There were many times when I would get up at one, two, or three in the morning after laying down at eleven at night, sometimes even later—it did not matter. This is the archetype for leaders who are in a high-performing and high-volume environment.

There was so much on my plate that often people would ask me how I managed it all. I would just readily smile with a head nod, to not ignore them. The reality of it all was that I was a hard worker. I was in before most and left after. I often carried a twenty-hour workday—yes, twenty hours—and it was a constant operation.

I went into the agency, intending to develop as a leader and excel. As I went higher in my supervisory and management roles, I was promoted in rapid succession. So rapidly I had reached the uniform rank of Assistant Chief while simultaneously holding the position of Deputy Chief of Staff, overseeing the operational data. As expected, when you rise in such an accelerated manner, things move fast and you do not initially digest all the processes around you, as it feels like a roller coaster ride with lots of speed, a big blur, and a huge thrill. Once the ride stabilizes and slows down at some point, you regain your bearings and reaffirm your surroundings. As my career slowed down, mostly because I had reached a pinnacle, I assessed my surroundings. I saw that some people around me had seen me differently; not because I had done anything in particular, but because people subconsciously created this divide where they felt I was not the same person they knew. That's always a difficult energy and transition to manage. However, I also realized I had developed opposition, not because of being promoted, but because I had become a formidable competitor. When people identify you as threatening to their position, they create a defensive attack. One day after being there for a few years, I was sitting in my office and I said to myself, "The same way I am getting applause is the same way I am getting hate."

Nothing had happened. No one had said or done anything to me when I had that thought. However, I knew the hate was there. Sometimes the hate had even disguised itself as applause. That may sound strange, but hate and jealousy are matching emotions. People are envious and sometimes it is that envy that drives people forward. Envy is their motivation.

In all honesty, many times systems are set up that way to use envy as ambition for competition. Leaders are ambitious and ambition is built upon the desire to succeed. Everyone cannot be successful at the same levels, so people become competitive. Once a team begins competing, the team members look at each other, analyzing each player and deciding who has what they want to achieve.

That's what's called our comparative nature. Someone sees another person's house and says, "I want to move over there because their house is bigger than mine." Once a person makes that decision, they do whatever they have to do to get what the other person has. Keeping up with the Joneses.

Envy sets in and, as much as we may not like it, envy is a motivating factor.

When I sat in my office that day, none of this had revealed itself, but I knew that hate was smart; it wouldn't come out until it was ready to strike. If I waited until then, it would be too late for me. Like my mother had told me, I had to be ready and brace for it.

In my situation, there came a point when my boss got tired of dealing with the unions. He didn't like that responsibility and whenever he had a union meeting, he would tell his secretary, "Find Sean and bring him in here." He brought me into every meeting. This was an important position because unions controlled so much, including the workforce of thousands of people.

I developed relationships with the men and women in the unions. I was dealing with people at all levels. The conversations sometimes went beyond business, talking about our families and our interests outside of the office. The more I dealt with the unions, the more favor I gained with them. Of course, that would happen. It's human nature. The more we deal with people, the more personal the relationship becomes.

As I came to know everyone, I had more of an edge in handling their issues. I became the problem solver. I got things done that would favor both parties. Even though I saw what was occurring and pushed back, the people from the unions only wanted to deal with me and less with my boss. That is what he wanted, right?

Even though my boss saw this happening, he ignored it because my working with the unions worked in his favor, leaving me in a very ugly situation. The politics of it all left me between a rock and a hard place. Anyone familiar with unions understands they are powerful and have overwhelming reach and influence. Imagine an unstoppable force meeting an immovable object. Either the commissioner or the union could have ended my career right where it stood had I not exhibited value as a medium. This was my daily work balance, and it was truly a high-wire act. See, powerful people, who are at opposite ends of an agenda, never continually want to deal directly with each other. They never want to allow the other person to learn them from such a close proximity. They always have a person who acts as a go-between, who allows them to save face. The last thing they want is for their opposition to get two bites at the apple. This is one of the reasons lawyers are so valued and powerful.

So, you can imagine what happened next. The commissioner realized I was garnering influence. After all, he was the commissioner.

He'd made this choice. He wanted me to do this. He'd given me the reins and because I had been a student who followed the moves of many before me, I was going to do a great job.

In these kinds of situations, people like my then-boss become angry, but they're angry at themselves. That's something they will never admit, so they divert that anger somewhere, to someone else. Looking back, I had made a huge mistake as well. I had allowed myself to become the treasurer.

I knew it wouldn't be long before the cards fell, and again, my mother's words rang in my ear. Because of that, I had silently begun to put an exit strategy in place. My plan was that if my boss or anyone turned on me, I didn't want to be in a situation where I would have to struggle to survive. I didn't want to be walked into a room, and, like Tommy in *Goodfellas*, find plastic on the floor. I needed to support my family with limited worries or concerns. I needed to develop a strategy that would allow me to survive the explosion, the uncontrollable, the unforeseen. A man or woman in a position of power must always have counselors. At the behest of the wisdom I had developed throughout my career, I sought counsel from two individuals whom I had grown to respect, not because of the positions they'd held, but because they had survived holding them.

Antonio was one of those counselors. He was one of the best-dressed and smoothest gents I worked with throughout my career. Antonio wasn't just a smooth cool dresser, though, he was also highly intelligent, and one of the few who understood the need for having an exit strategy. He understood the game, and he understood leadership.

Another one of my counselors that I often discussed strategies with was Warren. Now, Warren was truly a strategist and was battle-tested throughout his lengthy career. Having been in the crossfires of politics and leadership, he would always give a well-thought-out response, and I knew he would evaluate all options, leaving no stones unturned.

After discussing with my respected counselors, I started banking my time. I didn't get paid for overtime as a manager, but I could bank my compensatory time. I let it build up, keeping my strategy in mind—I needed one year: two thousand eighty-seven hours.

Sure enough, Mad Day came. That was the day when it all came out. People weren't happy with me anymore. Everything I had done wasn't good enough anymore. This is the time when you observe your friends become associates and your associates become enemies. When it was time for the powers that be to eliminate me, they were taken aback. I was prepared. Before anyone could say anything to me, I had enough compensatory time to take off under family leave. Once I enacted the leave, it placed me in a protective state that didn't allow me to be affected by the abusive influences that people in these situations are often subjected to. No one could touch me. My plan fully protected me.

Having an exit strategy is so important for a leader. You do yourself a disservice thinking your reign will never end. You must have a parachute because one thing that's true about leadership, you will never get out unscathed. An exit strategy allows you to leave with the least amount of damage, with your legacy somewhat intact, and your integrity and dignity in place.

That will only happen when you have your exit plan in place before it's time to leave.

CHAPTER 9

Your Word is Your Bond

In leadership, as in life, all you have is your word. Whatever your declaration, people need to believe your word. Your word is your value. Your word is the most important thing you can give. You're the vault and your words are the contents that gives it value. An empty vault is valueless when the contents inside are as well. Your word is gold, and I mean that literally. The more you've given your word and kept it, the more honor, credibility, and authority that will come with it.

Our ability to complete communication through verbal and body language, as well as our abilities to plot and plan strategically are what separates us from other species. We have these unique gifts, and we must treat and use them in that way. When you give your word—those who understand what that means value that. When people know your word means something, they will consider you and treat you as an equal.

When you give your word to people, based upon your actions, people decide its value—you just maintain it.

At one time, and this still exists in-some rare circles, a handshake was more valuable than a contract. When people looked each other in the eye, gave their word and shook hands, that action transcended all legalities. That action was a moral obligation and your credibility lay within that action.

While I am referring to this in professional terms, your word is as important on a personal level. If you're a person who says, "I'll be there at nine," but you show up at nine-thirty, people lose respect for your word and you lose credibility. Your word will no longer hold value—not only on what time you will arrive at a destination, but eventually, you will lose credibility in anything you say. Ultimately, you won't be able to garner an audience at all, because your vault won't have any value.

Here, I'm using time only as an example, but it's a good example. Let's say you said you were going to be somewhere at nine and then showed up half an hour later. Now, you've destroyed everything that will follow in time. You've planted a seed in bad soil and now your word has no value. More importantly, the missive in which you profess to lead would have just lost its followers.

Whenever I handled any kind of business, I made every effort to ensure I was in the position to give my word and then keep my word. It's important that you measure and mean what you're going to say before you say it. Sometimes you may not mean to lessen your value, but you will because you didn't consider other factors. Are there others who play a role that you do not control? Is this going to cause undue disruption to other operations outside of your influence? Will it draw abundant public pushback?

If the information you have at the time of commitment cannot bring you to a sound conclusion of surety, then it's just conjecture and not your word, which means you cannot completely give a guarantee. As a person who others may identify as an influential front-runner, the last thing you'd ever wish to do is box yourself into a position where you may not be able to keep your word.

If you're giving your word and it involves someone else, this is one situation that will often put you in a jam.

For example, if you tell someone, "I'll handle this contract. I'll have John change it," you've just given your word based on John's performance. In actuality, you may not have the authority or influence over John to give your word for him.

Then, when the change in the contract doesn't happen, it's on you. It's your credibility that is now questioned, even though it was John's performance, something over which you had no control. That is why you must be careful of how you speak. You don't always have to say, "I give you my word." You can say, "I'll make every effort." That is giving your word.

Your word being your bond is not just for you, but for others, and is a loaded charge just waiting to explode, especially as a leader. When you let people down too many times, when you fail them too often, they end up losing hope and belief in you altogether. This becomes crucial to your existence because it may prevent you from performing in the future. In leadership, you're only as good as your last performance and your last word.

So, if you say, "I'm going to reconstruct the school district," that's a huge task. That statement is firm. It is so absolute and doesn't leave any room or variation for failure. Once you give your word in that context, there's an expectation of qualification. People will assume you are qualified to do what you said you were going to do and, based on your word, they expect you will perform.

When you give your word, you are setting everyone else up for that performance, and if you don't keep your word, everything falls. Not only your performance, but everyone attached to you is affected. The only way this will not happen is if the people you have given your word to are smart enough to be strategic. If any of them have built-in mechanisms for failure, then they will have a backup plan that will not only save themselves, but just may save you as well.

There may be people who say, "Look, Mike said he'd take care of it and I believe him, but the 'trust-but-verify method' tells me I need to have something in place just in case Mike can't really do what he said he'd do."

It is just as important for you to be aware when others give their word. You must be strategic and have your Plan B so no one can take you down with them.

Understand that with people, there are no guarantees. No word, no strategy, no planning—nothing is one hundred percent. Saying what you mean and meaning what you say is such an important part of leadership. Once you've understood this part of leadership, you will speak with confidence and accuracy, and you will deliver.

Truthfulness is the Key

Numerous times I've been in multiple executive meetings where we covered the same subject because people couldn't pull off what they promised. They couldn't deliver what they said they were going to do. Most of the time, this happens because someone overpromised and wasn't completely truthful.

Truthfulness in its purest form is complete exposure because sometimes you may have to say you cannot meet expectations of a goal that was supposed to be achieved.

For example, I'm going to do a deal with someone, but first, I have to close one deal before I can get into a new one. Since I want to do business with this person, I say, "Victoria, I'm going to close this deal I'm working on, and then I'll give you $100,000 in a couple of days."

There are several challenges with this statement. First, how can I say this when I have not completed the deal I'm working on? Not only had I not completed the deal, but I also cannot one hundred percent guarantee the deal will ever be done, especially as the deal is still in progress.

However, because I don't want to lose the deal with Victoria, I'm selling her a dream. We sell dreams to people so we don't have to be truthful and can intentionally blind them. It is harder, without a doubt, but it is always better and more realistic to tell the truth. Within the truth lays a guarantee that manages expectations.

The best way to say it is, "Victoria, I'm working on this deal and although I'm confident it will go through, the reality is that the deal hasn't gone through yet. If and when I close the deal , you'll get the $100,000 so we can get started on our deal."

This is a much clearer and more truthful statement that will work for you and Victoria. You must realize, however, that by being truthful, you may open yourself up to vulnerabilities. There are a few things that become apparent with the latter statement to Victoria. First, the "if and when I close the deal" reveals that your relationship in your current deal may not be strong. Will that make Victoria change her mind about doing business with you? Will that make her move on to someone else whose money isn't contingent on someone else? Maybe.

I may lose the deal with Victoria by being truthful. However, it is better to do that than for me to give my absolute word on something that I cannot guarantee. In being truthful, Victoria still has my word—she will get the money if and when my deal closes. I gave her my word...with a qualifier, and I maintained my credibility.

The truth and that qualifier become important because many people won't do business with you if it gets around that your word isn't good. People won't even exchange a dollar with you if they don't believe you're being truthful, honest, or that you have integrity, all of which are attached to the value of your word.

Your word, even with a qualifier, makes people believe in you, makes people consistent with you, and makes people deal with you again. Your word gives you credit, which is what I call social credit that will lead to repeat business and new opportunities.

Never discount social credit, because just like financial credit, it has value. Sometimes someone has given their word to me and they didn't come through. When that happens, I have the option of evaluating their value to me—their social credit. Their word has just been compromised and I have to determine if they yield any further value. However, if they had social credit with me and had built up value from past situations, in some instances I determined it was worth maintaining the relationship. Other times, not so much. You have to make that determination as to the value of continuing the relationship.

In those instances when someone gave me their word and it didn't happen, and those individuals had social credit with me, I knew for sure that when they hadn't come through, there was nothing else they could have done to make it happen. I trusted they put everything into trying to get it done, but for whatever reason, it did not come through. I was good with that because of the social credit they had with me.

However, like financial credit, social credit is spent. What you want to do is always remain credit-worthy.

Taking Your Word Back

You've read all I had to say about keeping your word. However, here's the twist. As with all things in this world, nothing is ever one hundred percent. It is said you should expect the worst and hope for the best. Believe it or not, and with all you've read about keeping your word, sometimes going back on your word is fair and acceptable. These instances should specifically surround your family, health, and circumstances that would cause your professional or personal lifestyle to be destroyed. No commitment is ever worth personal or professional destruction. The well-being of you and your family is of utmost importance.

The first rule of life is self-preservation, which includes your word. If you gave your word with good faith and intention, and then information came to you that wasn't readily available when you gave your word, then having to change it is acceptable. However, understand that when committing to anyone regarding anything, there will always be a purgatory period of the X-factor, all of which is unknown. There's always a chance that something could occur, the introduction of new information that could make the commitment null and void. This happens regularly with negotiations of legal contracts under what would be known as a "good faith clause." This simply means that both parties have negotiated with sincerity and honesty based on the information that was known at the time.

Occasionally, extenuating circumstances will keep you from keeping your word. Suppose a leader's partner is due to give birth in the next three weeks. Based on that medical prediction, they've set up all of their projects to be completed before then. They've considered everything, made their plans, given their word, and then, the night before they were to deliver on a major project, they received a call while in their office.

"Honey...."

From the sound of their partner's voice, they know something's up. They're having the baby now. The leader drops everything because there is only one thing on their mind, only one concern.

This is a hypothetical situation, but like many other situations, it is very real. No matter how important the presentation you were to give, no matter how important the document you were supposed to deliver, your personal situation trumps it all.

That is a fact of life. We have professional priorities, but it is unrealistic to think we don't have personal priorities as well. There is no way to plan for everything; extenuating circumstances will prevent you from keeping your word. However, as a leader, you have built up the respect and leadership equity to where others will be very understanding during these times.

CHAPTER 10

The Cost of Leadership

There's an old saying, "To get to heaven, first you must die." Now, yes, those words, while true, may sound extreme, but think about it. To yield the rewards of your journey, you must do things many are not willing to do. I've discussed that you never leave leadership unscathed. There's a penalty, a cost that comes with leadership that everyone must consider. People want to be leaders, but that's because many only see the glorified aspects of it. However, glory is not what leadership is about. That's not the authenticity of leadership.

Leadership comes with a lot. For one, failure and vicarious liability because you're responsible for everything, even if you don't know about it. If someone is under your tutelage—if their name is under yours on the organizational chart—you are responsible for them and all the actions that come along with them being under your purview. This makes you the face of the agency, which can be a heavy load to bear. Over time, all that weight will take its toll. You are the representation of all successes and all failures. You have to understand the value and the devaluation of it.

Leadership can also be a very lonely place. Like Colin Kaepernick found out, sometimes you take a position to gain nothing and lose everything. That happens in superhero movies all the time. A character may say, "I'm okay with dying as long as the rest of the team takes everything forward for the win."

Being scathed is a part of leadership. You will not leave the same way you came in, and that's a guarantee. You will lose something: your credibility, integrity, finances, marriage, or children. Others have lost their souls, or, far worse, their lives. There's an entire gamut of things on the table that you may lose when you step into the realm of leadership.

The price of leadership extends beyond your business or organization. It goes right into your personal life. When you have a high-powered leadership position, it will take its toll at home. It's as the Bible says in Matthew 6:24: *"You can't serve two masters. Either you will hate the one and love the other, or you will be devoted to the one and despise the other..."* Simply, to be loyal to one is to betray the other. The juggle of both will surely leave instability.

All titans eventually become targets. It is because of this reason, and all I stated above, that you must go into leadership with your eyes wide open. This will allow you to manage potential losses better. Never be foolish in thinking there won't be any losses. Knowing that there will be a cost at home, you can pay more attention to your significant others and loved ones. Because you know the demands of what you will have to put into play, you can better measure and navigate your ability to minimize your failures.

So now, a husband may bring home flowers more often, or a wife may get tickets to her husband's favorite show. Or you may say that once a week, though, you may have to be flexible with the night, you will have dinner together no matter what. When you know the costs, you can manage your expenses better, you can discuss them ahead of time, and put a plan into place that will yield you the best results as a leader and as a loved one.

That is what leadership is all about—strategic planning, even at home.

CHAPTER 11

Success Exists in Uncomfortable Places

We can measure the road to success best through comfortability or lack thereof; the more uncomfortable the situation, the greater potential for success. The greater the success, the greater the reward, personally, professionally, and financially. There is no success without struggle. For struggle is the only gateway to that destination. It's almost a proclamation that controversy will precede every big win. This is true in almost any industry.

It's often said that when people are talking about you, both positively or negatively, that's a good thing; you've just got to make sure they spell and pronounce your name right. The flip side of this is when no one is talking about you, you're not relevant. You're not making an impact.

Relevancy can be uncomfortable because when you're in that space, although there's plenty of space to build you up, there is just as much space to tear you down. Please make no doubt about it, folks will come for you, and it won't take too much time either. It is said that the same things that make you laugh will make you cry. Think about this in its most practical form, the seasons. Winter can be our most brutal time of the year. It's the harshest of all seasons. There isn't any growth of vegetation. Frost covers the plains, and the conditions overall can destroy the very existence of life itself. Winter, by far, compared to the other seasons, has the most unbearable impact on life. Those who can endure and survive those harsh winter conditions will bear witness to the beauty of summer. The warmth of the sun, the visions of beautiful flower-covered landscapes, and that favorite calm, passive breeze. Comparing winter to summer demonstrates the uncomfortable period and the success that follows.

Success is your payment for surviving hard decisions and making tough choices that could cost you your career. You have to sign off on those things that other people are afraid to sign off on because sometimes that signature will bring some sharp teeth.

Leadership is all about outcomes, and every time you elevate, every time you're promoted, and you're responsible for more people, more issues will come your way, more liabilities, and more potential disasters. These are uncomfortable things, but that's where you will find success, in the uncomfortable places. That's also where you find loyalty, where you find the new leaders, and those unpolished diamonds, you can mentor into a shining gem.

CHAPTER 12

Progress is More Valuable Than Movement

I once worked with John, a high-level chief and an executive who was in the office twenty-plus hours a day. That's not an exaggeration. Many nights, John wouldn't go home and would sleep in his car. He was so passionate about his work, so completely involved in everything.

Everything about the picture John painted physically showed his extreme dedication to the job. Anyone who saw and interacted with him, couldn't help but be impressed with that level of movement and activity—a true, dedicated company employee.

John moved around and was busy, and busier. However, there was one major problem: his movement wasn't qualifying his existence in his position. He wasn't getting the job done. Back in the day, this was called "busy work" and he had plenty of that, but the deeper you looked at him and his assignments, the more you saw he wasn't influential. He hadn't mastered the task.

Management didn't notice John wasn't accomplishing, which was an even bigger problem. He was here, there, and everywhere, always giving the visual perception of progress. Yet the numbers didn't lie and there was never any change. He was like a hamster running on a wheel—in the same spot, running and running, the wheel spinning and spinning. Nothing changes until the hamster realizes it needs to get off, and that's usually for some food or some other natural distracting goal.

However, this person wasn't consciously connected to the fact that the numbers weren't good. By constantly staying in motion, John cleared his conscience. He believed that because of all of his motion, progress would eventually come. He believed that in the end, he would have that necessary win.

In the end, however, nothing happened at all. He had shown up, but never accomplished his mission. Sadly, this executive didn't realize this truth until it was too late… not until the company let him go. Because so many people confuse activity for productivity, it's a hard transition to make. However, all movement is not progressive. When progress is made, it's known, it's clear, it's undeniable. Progress identifies and qualifies itself. As a leader, you will never have to go into a meeting or make a presentation to sell progress. Progress sells itself.

Here's another truth about movement and progression that leaders must know: Every person who leads a movement isn't always the one who can progress it. As a leader, know that you may not be the best or most beneficial person to lead a movement or a project. That revelation may not always come in the beginning. You may start a project, and then see that while there is movement, there are no results. When that happens, a strong leader will first look at their current course of action to analyze and evaluate what needs to change. In some instances, the change in direction may need to be a pruning of the team or a relinquishing of a team member's role. Maybe the passing of the torch is needed to complete the mission with the best results.

It is difficult for a leader to do this. People may construe this action as giving up or failing. The leader may not want to let anyone else in for fear of losing the credit if the project does well, or even for fear of having the project taken away. Any person in a position of leadership who takes the fear approach will set themselves up for failure. There are only two positions in life: forward or reverse, increase or decline, either progression or death. Movement without progression is sure death. For even idleness is a purgatory.

That's why moving the project along with another person, who is the best person, is something that must happen for the greater good. Choosing to step aside and allowing another to come in is a decision that shows the maturity that comes along with the experience of leadership.

The bottom line is this: activity is no indicator of productivity. Focus on results, so you can receive the rewards.

Then do what is necessary to get those results and rewards. Too often, employees confuse their dedication to the organization with being dedicated to the organization's mission. This may sound strange, but leadership's dedication should never be to the organization but to the organization's ability to create successful outcomes. Organizations are only as successful as the creatives within them. Meaning, that once you become dedicated to the organization itself, the organization becomes your leader.

Instead of consciously doing all that's necessary to make the company a success, you now do enough to keep yourself and the company together. It becomes less about the mission and more about your relationship with power. You never want it to go away, and the growth in both the employee and the organization ceases and continues in a state of non-advancement. Those who don't attach to the organization per se, but to its outcomes, continue with a driven mindset of forward-thinking and forward action. Never forget the ultimate endgame, which inevitably is to be a profitable, successful, and growth-nurturing environment.

CHAPTER 13

The Importance of Counsel

No matter how educated you are, no matter how much experience you have, no matter how you've risen in your company or organization, you must have counsel. You must have someone who will pull your coattails and tell you the real deal, or you will most certainly fail. This counsel has nothing to do with education, nor does it have anything to do with legalities. This has to do with the maturity of those who have, through their practical experience in life, proven to have gained the knowledge, wisdom, and understanding to make sound decisions.

Never underestimate the value of someone who you cannot only talk to but listen to as well. Even people who are counselors for a living, like attorneys, have counsel. When a lawyer gets into any kind of legal situation, the first action is to hire someone else. Even lawyers know that any attorney who defends himself has a fool for a client.

To succeed, a contrary opinion is necessary. You must have a difference and a deference of opinion. You must be able to hear someone who can speak to you about the other side. This counsel can add light to your opinion, to your ideas, to your mission. The key is that you must be open to hearing and accepting. You cannot shoot down the elements of support that are there to build you up. You must hear, you must listen.

This seems like a simple concept, but some leaders believe they always know best. They are usually unwilling or unable to comprehend the law of inclusion. They block out other voices, and won't listen to anyone. That kind of thinking is a quick pathway to failure.

Good counsel is necessary for every industry. For example, the entertainment industry. Let's say, hypothetically, there was an actress whose career started as a comedian. She did well with her comedy act on the road, ended up with a highly rated sitcom television show, and secured a role in a major movie that won her critical acclaim. No doubt, this actress saw her star rising—after all, she was extremely talented. Her family life was intact and all of life's trees were bearing fruit from her hard work and dedication.

For the first part of her career, she made wise choices. Then, she found herself in a situation with a major studio regarding a movie she was contracted to star in. In an unfavorable decision toward the studio, she decided not to follow the rules of the game, even though the studio was putting a lot of money behind her. They had already invested a substantial amount of money and they needed her to promote their project.

She didn't want to do it. She thought, because of her success, she was in a positive, comfortable financial situation, where she could pay her mortgage and other bills with ease, and, thus, followed her own rules. However, she didn't have enough money to buck the system, not that way. As such, the studio decided to sever ties.

That one decision began an avalanche that ended up costing her much of her career, but one that good counsel could have prevented if she'd listened to other voices. Someone who could have sat her down and helped her measure the costs of her decision to not go along with the studio's requests. Someone should have gone through the pros and the cons with her, as well as helped her to think about what her decision could mean in the future.

Here, one would think that her husband may have jumped in to counsel her because, even though she was a successful actress, her business affected everyone in the household. He would have as much to lose by a bad decision as she did. He had a vested interest; her business was now the family business.

Their situation was like a lot of television shows and movies where one character says to another, "If I go down, so do you." The characters are talking about having a vested interest in each other.

Of course, no one truly knows the internal family dynamics in this actress's situation, and one wouldn't want to know, but it doesn't appear as if she had much help. It seems she studied her choices, made a decision, and then went with what she wanted to do. That was her right. Once she did that, though, the studio had a choice of what they were going to do, which was their right! Not just that studio; others in the industry decided not to continue to work with her. The skinny of this example is that the consequences of your decisions can be heavy, and although you may continue down the path of your own volition and make the same impactful decision, having exercised your counsel will bring reassurance that your decision was mature and considerably engaged. Those who understand the importance of counsel make choices that are usually qualifying to the issue at hand and are the least charged with emotion.

One of the most important things to note is that "good counsel" can come from anyone of personal trust, who has an unbiased and unvested interest. When we hear counsel, we automatically often think of attorneys, and that is true for corporations and organizations. Often, they have dozens, and sometimes more, depending on the size of the organization, to take care of their corporate issues — that's the importance of counsel. Even the White House has attorneys who serve as counselors, guiding and directing the president and the White House staff.

In other situations, we don't always need attorneys. Spouses, mentors, other family members, and anyone who will tell you the truth can play the same role. Think about the counsel we've all received from our mothers and grandmothers. For most of us, their guidance and counsel have been priceless, even though they may not have any education in the industry that we're in. Principles are usually the same across all industries.

However, those people in our lives who love us and want to see us do well have a vested interest in helping us do the right thing. They want to see us win, and because of our history with our mothers, grandmothers, and others, it's easy for us to listen to them.

Sit down with your counsel and hear their voices, even when it's hard, even when you want to disagree. You must be able to sit down, knowing that the only reason you will listen to them is that you trust them. You must trust your counsel or else they can never serve you well in that capacity. Listen, learn, and know that every leader needs a counselor.

It is still important to note, though, that the final decision belongs to you as the leader. Yes, you should have and must listen to counsel, and hear all sides. However, the buck stops with you.

A great example of this is the ultimate leader—the President of the United States. When President Obama received intel that Osama bin Laden was hiding out in Pakistan, the president had a huge judgment he had to make. The intel wasn't one hundred percent guaranteed. Remember, nothing is one hundred percent. Even if bin Laden was there, President Obama didn't know what our Navy Seals would face. The Navy Seals could go in and lose their lives. There was a chance that Osama bin Laden would not have been there at all and that would have greatly damaged our country's relationship with Pakistan.

President Obama called in his entire team. He listened to all sides. From the vice president to the secretary of defense, the secretary of state, and others in his cabinet, President Obama asked for honest counsel from every member of his team, and that's a hard thing to trust.

Then, once all sides are heard, the burden of the decision lay with the leader. It was President Obama who said that he had to go off by himself and weigh everything he'd heard. He'd listened, he considered, and then, as the leader, he made the decision.

It turned out to work (almost) perfectly. One of our country's greatest enemies was captured and killed. However, it could have gone the other way as well. That didn't matter to the leader. President Obama listened to his important counsel—then himself—and then he made the final decision.

A leader doesn't have to feel as if he or she is out there alone. With good counsel on your team, there will be people who will have your back. Making final decisions, however, can be a lonely place. The buck has to stop with you!

That is why it's important to be in the right frame of mind when making decisions. Never make a decision out of disparity or anger and never make a permanent decision as a means to satisfy a temporary issue. Decisions carry great risks, but they can also carry great rewards.

That is why every bit has to be measured and why counsel is so important. Leadership decisions are the things that make careers. They are the foundation of your success. Decide wisely...and with good counsel.

CHAPTER 14

Purpose and Cause

Occasionally, a leader may wander without a purpose and be stuck in a state of cause. Depending on circumstances, responsibilities, and expectations, that will probably be bad for the leader and worse for those who are following.

Let me define these terms: Purpose is *an ending or a goal.* Cause is *how that goal gets started or is influenced to be continued.* A cause will motivate you and a purpose will inspire you.

Here's an example: You're in Orlando, Florida, and a friend calls you and asks if you want to take a ride and you say, "Sure!" When they arrive, you get in the car with them. Since this is a good friend whom you trust, you may not ask a lot of questions. You just hop in. You don't know where you're going. You're just along for the ride.

However, as the trip progresses, you become curious. Still, you don't have any idea where you're going or what this journey is about. You don't know the destination, but you have a bond with the driver and trust your friend has your best interests at heart.

The trip continues for a while and you doze off. When you wake up, you see a sign announcing that you're in Miami, Florida, about three hours away from your starting point.

Now, a light bulb goes off in your mind. You have more information. At least you know one purpose of the trip—to go to Miami.

Then, your friend says to you, "I wanted to bring you to Miami because I hit the lotto and I'm going to cash this check, then give you a couple of dollars."

Now you have an even clearer understanding of the entire journey. Now you know the *purpose*.

Can you imagine, however, being on that same trip and never finding out where you're going? Never finding out why you're in that car? That's the way it is for many people in leadership. Men and women end up in positions in companies, organizations, agencies, and institutions, and they're miserable because they don't know why they're there. They're only existing where they are because they haven't understood their purpose.

Even in a family, everyone has their purpose. Families are set up like a business with laws and moral structures. Think about it: a family has a CEO, a vice president, and a treasurer.

In some families, the same person plays several roles, but the structure is there, and everyone knows their role and their purpose.

Even in a two-person relationship, there has to be a structure. Whenever I talk with people about relationships, I tell them, "They build most door frames for one person to go through at a time. Can you imagine two people trying to walk through the entryway at the same time? That might hurt!"

The needs and demands will determine who goes through the door first. I want to make a note here: the leader can be a man or a woman.

It's the understanding of the purpose that alleviates a lot of the issues, negativity, and pressures that exist from not knowing what the journey is all about. It eliminates the questions: Why am I here? Why do I exist? Why do they need me?

It is only when you understand your purpose that you become your purpose. You must know it before you become it, and becoming it is what the journey is all about. Whether it's your life journey, the institutional journey, or the leadership journey where you're ascending higher, it's all about purpose.

Purpose is beyond the job description. Your job description defines your tasks, but your purpose is greater than that. Your purpose is your reason for being there. Why did this organization, corporation, agency, or institution bring you in before anyone else? What is your purpose? What is it you're supposed to do, supposed to accomplish?

These are questions that very few take the time to study and answer because we live in a microwave society where many people rush into situations, not wanting to take any time to sit back and analyze. Even in our conversations, we're rushing, sometimes answering the other person before they've completely asked the question. "Oh, I know, I know," is what people often say, queued up to respond before processing the information they just received.

To have maximum success, you have to stop. You have to sit down, take your time, and understand what is going on so you can understand your complete role and the reasons beyond the job description.

To truly understand the purpose, you must first understand the dynamics of the journey. Unlike that trip example, you must gather all the information before the journey, because that is what will give you what you need to proceed with intelligence and wisdom. Of course, this will take time. You cannot develop intelligence and wisdom without patience. You must watch, hear, and absorb all the information, reading what's going on—including studying body language, which is sometimes up to ninety percent of our communication.

One thing I put a lot of my focus on was studying how to go into a room and read it. I'd learned this during my early years of life growing up in New York City. I could see someone approaching from a block away and could decipher whether trouble was coming. Most people who grew up in big urban cities can, especially true New Yorkers. I had honed my skills in that area on the streets when I was young. So, I knew what to do during my professional adult years, and how to apply it. When I walked in, I listened to what they said, heard how they said it, and watched their body language and interaction with each other. I spent more time watching and listening than speaking. I never wanted to lead a conversation unless I was the one presenting. Otherwise, I waited until everyone else spoke so I could get a full, not partial, understanding of the dynamics in the room. I wanted to know who were the alpha personalities, where were the challenges, who were the quiet ones, and which ones were the most boisterous. What I wanted to know was how the room rotated on its axis.

Leaders should always evaluate their leadership globe. Where's the land as opposed to the bodies of water? Where are the swamps as opposed to the desert? Who are your allies and who are your enemies? Only by knowing the lay of the land can you understand your purpose, and how to use all the resources available to you to ensure you fulfill that purpose. Those resources are the passengers in the vehicle you're driving, who will travel to unknown destinations without a complete understanding of where they're going or how they're going to get there. They're just riding with you because they know you have a purpose.

CHAPTER 15

Team Building

When a new leader walks into an organization or corporation, it is with the thought that they are there because the company is not up to par. They believe they're coming in to bring something new, to add, to change, and restructure.

Most times, that understanding is true. However, what needs to be added, changed, or restructured needs to come after an evaluation is done. It should not and cannot be something automatic and instantaneous.

Leaders want to walk through the door and positively change the world and that's an admirable quality. However, it's a mistake that's often made in leadership because by doing that, by walking in and making changes, that leader is speaking for the people who are already there. That leader is saying he or she knows what's best and is already speaking this organization's language.

In actuality, the leader doesn't know the language at all. The leader just got there and has had no time to learn it. The leader has to learn everything about that organization's infrastructure and culture first. Questions need to be asked and answered: What is the culture? How do they speak? What is the atmosphere like? What are the nuances? For the leader, it will be like peeling back the layer of an onion, and the more you peel, the more that's revealed. Although it may look the same, it will have a definite dramatic tearing effect.

The initial analysis that the leader must do is like a medical examination. When going to a doctor, you don't walk into the office and have the doctor immediately perform surgery. Of course not. First, the doctor does an examination: taking your height, weight, and blood pressure before they move on to blood tests. Then, they do an evaluation and maybe a few tests, and analyze all the collected information.

The doctor goes through these steps first because he doesn't know what's wrong with you before an examination and evaluation. Surgery cannot be a recommendation until he knows all the issues and can weigh the varying outcomes.

Like a doctor, a leader has to first determine the culture before you can create a strategic plan. The first step is to realize that you need a team. A team is necessary. None of us is greater than the sum of all parts. None of us can do any major project or accomplish any major goals alone. When you bring together a group of people (professionally in a company or organization, or personally with a family), all parties involved must understand that the team is the strongest entity there is.

Once you realize you need a team, the next step is to plan who you will bring to your team. The plan is the starting point. It is there where you must ask yourself these key questions: Who do you need? What roles do you want each member to play? What will be each team member's purpose? What is the realistically intended outcome for each team member?

These huge questions must be answered before you can clean house. You must know these answers before you can remove the current team and bring in your own people. With that said, absent of any scandal or destructive issues, bringing in your own people at the very beginning is not always a good move. How can a leader dismiss anyone when the leader has no real sense of who's who? A leader who does this most likely has made a hugely negative and sometimes irreversible decision without knowing crucial facts: Where are the loyalties? What are the prior relationships? What are the team's dynamics—its strengths and weaknesses?

When walking into a new situation, as a leader, alter or adjust your team in phases. Think of it this way: if you're an interior decorator hired to redecorate a home, you cannot go into the home and rearrange the furniture without having first interviewed the people who live there. This has become a dangerous trend in leadership. For example, someone newly appointed to lead will go into an organization, clean house, and hire people from everywhere but from that state, and that leader believes the team they've chosen will go into the organization in an unfamiliar environment and run things. How? This leader and the new team don't even understand the culture of the respective organization. They don't know the energy or the dynamics. They know nothing about people who were part of that corporation or organization. Suffice to say, they won't even have the political relationships needed to make organizational changes, and believe me, they will need those relationships.

Sometimes, it's not bringing people in from other parts of the country but bringing in a team from other industries. New leaders will often make this mistake as well. Just because someone was a great criminal justice professor, does not mean they will do well as a law enforcement officer. Now, of course, this is not absolute. Yes, some brilliant people may offer efficient production and intelligent ideas to the environment. Many times, when there is a change, of course, the environment may need an introduction of new ideas. However, the change should always be inclusively mended with the culture of the current residence input: both physical and mental.

If you ever find yourself in a situation and you're wondering why the team isn't gelling, why people are not seeing your vision, or why your agenda is not moving forward, ask yourself these questions: What did you do to change the team? Did you overturn the dynamics? One thing that's important to note about changing out people: once you remove someone from the team, they cannot be brought back. So, make these kinds of changes wisely.

It may not be that you didn't connect to the people. Maybe you tried to change too much. Of course, you're going to change out some people and bring in your own, but for the sake of the foundation that is already there, you must have a balance. Look at the situation and decide what percentage of people will stay and who will have to leave. It's important, though, to know that to achieve your agenda, some of the foundation should remain in place. Some nuances exist in corporations, organizations, agencies, etc. There will be things you won't know as an outsider and things that will take you too long to learn. You need part of the old team around you.

Understand, though, that this is a tough decision to make. In a casino, the dealer's loyalty is to the house. People who remain have loyalties to those who were there before you. You won't know where these loyalties lie, which is why you must be aware, observant, and open.

I remember a situation when I worked with the New York City Department of Correction. One day, I learned that the commissioner was upset because he'd heard that the chief of the Department, who was the highest-ranking uniform person in the agency, allegedly had said something about him. It got to the commissioner's ego so much that he called a meeting, wanting the chief to appear in his office and answer for the rumors.

However, the commissioner didn't want the chief alone. He wanted several key members of his executive staff present. In the office, the commissioner confronted the chief.

"I need people who are loyal, people who believe in me. And I've heard that you've been saying these things about me. I want to know if that's true."

The chief didn't take the commissioner's questioning well. He told the commissioner, "I'm a man. I don't have to repeat my conversations with anybody. If I needed you to know what I said, you'd know it." He went on to say, "I'm not going to have a professional conversation about a rumor."

Because he was new to the agency, the commissioner was unaware of the existing respect between several members of the executive staff and the chief. The commissioner had called a meeting where he thought he had his team with him. Unfortunately, the commissioner didn't know that some of his staff in the room were on the other side. The chief turned the commissioner's intimidation into a bluff.

He would not win this encounter because he didn't even know the players on the chessboard. He didn't know who was in the room. The relationships formed before he became commissioner, even outside of the agency were strong, but the commissioner didn't know that. He held a meeting and didn't even know who was on whose side. Everyone had the drop except for him.

Knowing these kinds of things gives people the advantage when assembling and building a team. There is no way for you to know everything. However, if you build your team right, you will have a person who's, what I call, the epicenter, and the goal is for this person to have a pretty good relationship with most of their peers both politically and in some instances socially. He or she doesn't have to be friends with the entire team. They just have to get people to the table to have the relevant conversations that you may need. As the epicenter, that person needs to know the environment, so he or she can help you keep your pulse on the team, can be your advance man/woman, letting you know when things are coming your way, or giving you a heads-up about things you should know or look out for.

When you're entering a new company and building a team, find your epicenter. That is imperative. He or she will be critical to your success.

Eventually, I played that role for the commissioner. I believe that was one of the reasons he chose me for the position. I had a great level of influence and likeability that I had garnered through my time with the agency, and have been able to help many professionally as they matured through their careers. He watched me after he met me when I was an assistant deputy warden, which is equivalent to the rank of lieutenant in the police department. I was young and energetic, and he liked all of that about me.

After a few encounters, the commissioner sent word for me to interview for the recently vacant deputy chief of staff position. Before he sent word, though, he did his due diligence, discovering that I had professional relationships with lots of people. I worked in the public and media relations office for over a decade, and public relations is all about relationships. Understanding that, he knew I would be able to not only translate information when he needed it, but I'd be able to add clout to him through his transition as the new leader in the agency. I would be able to be a bridge or extend an olive branch when needed, and also validate his credibility by telling people, "The commissioner is good!" Even if it was just a visual assumption from having me on the team.

I was a strong communicator; I had even stronger relationships. I could read a room, understand energy and body language, and I was determined to get the job done. All of those things made me a great epicenter.

The key to choosing an epicenter is that the person must be someone you trust. They don't have to have a string of degrees or be an attorney. They just must be someone you can speak to intelligently; someone you can bounce ideas off of and know for sure they're not just going to be your yes-person. You have to trust this person enough to come into your office, close the door, and say, "Hey, listen, I know this is what was said in the meeting, but I want you to think about these other things." You cannot be afraid to hear it, and your epicenter can't be afraid to say it.

The epicenter is your anchor, and without the anchor, the rest of your team is irrelevant. There will be times in the organization where the middle will move, the dial on the spectrum will change, and you may lose your position—maybe not technically, but figuratively. In this situation, who will be there to help you? To help you reset? Who is your reset person?

One last thing about the epicenter, the anchor of your team; I've discussed all the attributes this person should have, but there is one thing that you must know as you make your selection. Make sure you understand the ambitions of the person you choose. You're going to be bringing this person into your circle and the last thing you want is to create a situation where you're building up your competition. So, make sure you're aware of the goals and objectives of the person you're bringing close to you. Again, it's about trust and you're going to have to measure trust against their skill sets. Both are equally important.

The commissioner knew my goals and knew that I wanted to do much more with my career. So, after evaluating me, he decided I was a good choice for the position. I knew I'd be his epicenter; that would be my role. I would help him with the team and also assist him if he ever needed a reset. One of my strengths was understanding a team was more than a group of people. I had developed an ability to look at the individuals and see the value that each person brought to the team. To determine value, I gave people tests to perform and waited to see what results they returned.

What's interesting about value, however, is that it differs for everyone. For example, I had a boss who saw value in movement, and, based on what was discussed in earlier chapters, movement is nothing more than activity. It has nothing to do with productivity. However, when I worked for the commissioner, he saw value in high-energy individuals. What I knew, though, is that leaders come in more than one package. Yes, high energy can be a good attribute, but so can low energy, because that person may be very focused. The key is to find the gems in people based on who they are.

It is that understanding that I use when building a team. I know also that a team is more than a group of people. A team is about individual relationships. I always wanted to know more than the names and resumes of the people on the team. I wanted to know who they were as individuals. Their work habits. What they liked and disliked: Oh, do you like coffee, or do you prefer lattes? Do you like scones or would you prefer doughnuts?

Those are just examples, but I use them to show how you must go beyond the resume. I wanted to know where they were from. What were their family dynamics? What were their goals? Those things may seem small, but they are points on a roadmap. They tell a story about the person. Those are the details that help you connect and that was my goal, to connect with as many people as I could on the team.

However, it was more than just my belief in building relationships that the commissioner admired about me. While I was always kind and assertive as a leader, I was also very honest, too. The commissioner used to always say, "Well, we know Sean has no hair on his tongue."

That was the truth. I had no challenges speaking what I thought and telling people what they needed to hear. If I was going to open my mouth and contribute, I was going to talk, but not with fluff. I would get right to the point.

That is necessary for leadership, but not something that you will always find. Often, I'd sit in meetings for an hour while twelve other people tap-danced around an issue.

After everyone had their turn to speak, I'd jump in with the critical action questions. We had a major project in one of the jails. We were two weeks from opening a new wing designed to rehabilitate, change, and restructure the behavior of some of the most violent incarcerated individuals. The wing was built with lots of new concepts: there were net caging and cubicles where four and five of these violently assaultive individuals could recreate. Officers would be able to move around but would be separated, so there was less risk of being assaulted.

This was a big project and a huge accomplishment for the city and the agency as the violent assaults on staff were increasing. In that meeting two weeks before opening, I had the impression that people were tap dancing around what we needed to discuss. No one was talking about the necessary staffing needed to operate such a unit. It was like one of those issues that people were going to close their eyes and hoped went away, but never does. In environments of this nature with a high potential for hostility, the proper staffing—security and programming, as well as staffing levels—are of utmost importance.

So, after everyone had their say, I asked the critical question: "Do we have a listing of the staff? Everyone? Do we have a list of all the program staff?"

It was quiet for a couple of seconds as everyone looked at each other. Then finally, someone spoke up. "We're working on it. We're still putting it together."

I was incredulous. I said, "So, you mean we sat here for a whole hour and went through all of this and we don't have staffing?"

It amazed me that no one else had asked that question. That should have been asked first. Staffing was the most important part of this project. There is no rehabilitation without the rehabilitators. How could the place open without people?

This let me know a couple of things: yes, we had a team, but we didn't have the right people in each position and that was going to be a problem because the team reflected the commissioner. The less efficient a member of the team is, the more the other members must carry the burden of additional responsibility. Therefore, the team leader and their leadership choices are extremely important. Who they choose for the team, and how they influence them to do it, makes all the difference.

So, when you're a leader and selecting that point person, your epicenter, you must choose someone who will look at the whole picture for you. Someone who will help you build a good team, and who will have a hawk-eye view of not only the team but all the projects as well. Your epicenter should be able to help you attain maximum results.

LEADERSHIP IS KING!

Whether you're an emerging leader or a veteran, this book gives you tools and strategies you can use in any kind of business or industry. Today's business climate is dynamic, constantly changing with new methods and technologies, and that type of environment demands great leaders. The key to leadership is to remain relevant by continually evolving and growing. It is important to recognize your leadership strengths and weakness. Learning to reinforce your weaknesses, while propelling forward to greater heights on those attributes that are your strengths, will be the leadership quality that those who follow you will respect the most. This will inevitably become your body of work, your legacy.

Leadership is not always easy, but it can always be rewarding for you and those on your team. Your focus should be on the things that can transform you and your organization to improve performance, have a meaningful impact, and produce favorable results. *Leadership is King* is one tool that can help enhance your intelligence on the subject of leadership.

FAVORITE QUOTES

"Don't confuse efforts with results, as everything is impossible until someone does it."
– Sean F. Jones

"Success. Its got enemies. You can be successful and have enemies or you can be unsuccessful and have friends."
– American Gangster film, 2007

"One will never rise above the plain of their mentality. Grow your mind!"
– Sean F. Jones

"Most people fail in life not because they aim too high and miss, but because they aim too low and hit."
– Les Brown

"One must hear in order to listen, and understand in order to learn."
– Sean F. Jones

"Success is nothing more than a few simple disciplines, practiced every day."
– Jim Rohn

"A dream remains a dream until you bring it to life and make it a vision, but both must be present to attain a goal."
– Sean F. Jones

"Change the way you look at things and the things you look at will change."
– Wayne Dyer

"There aren't any secrets to success only systems."
– Sean F. Jones

"Don't make excuses make adjustments."
– Eric Thomas

"*You don't have to be great to get started, but you have to get started to be great.*"
– Zig Ziglar

"*Success only exists in uncomfortable places.*"
– Sean F. Jones

"*People do not decide their futures, they decide their habits and their habits decide their futures.*"
– F. M. Alexander

"*Courage is going from failure to failure without losing enthusiasm.*"
– Winston Churchill

"*Never let anyone know what you are thinking until its to the benefit of your necessity.*"
– Sean F. Jones

"*Sometimes the bravest and most important thing you can do is just show up.*"
– Brene' Brown

'*A great leader's courage to fulfill their vision comes from passion, not position.*"
– John C. Maxwell

www.ingramcontent.com/pod-product-compliance
Lightning Source LLC
Chambersburg PA
CBHW021220130726
47988CB00002B/743